teach®
yourself

basic computer skills

Windows XP edition

moira stephen

teach yourself
70
1938 2008
celebrate with us

Launched in 1938, the **teach yourself** series grew rapidly in response to the world's wartime needs. Loved and trusted by over 50 million readers, the series has continued to respond to society's changing interests and passions and now, 70 years on, includes over 500 titles, from Arabic and Beekeeping to Yoga and Zulu. What would you like to learn?

Be where you want to be with **teach yourself**

For UK order enquiries: please contact Bookpoint Ltd, 130 Milton Park, Abingdon, Oxon OX14 4SB. Telephone: +44 (0)1235 827720. Fax: +44 (0)1235 400454. Lines are open 09.00–17.00, Monday to Saturday, with a 24-hour message answering service. Details about our titles and how to order are available at www.teachyourself.co.uk.

For USA order enquiries: please contact McGraw-Hill Customer Services, PO Box 545, Blacklick, OH 43004-0545, USA. Telephone: 1-800-722-4726. Fax: 1-614-755-5645.

For Canada order enquiries: please contact McGraw-Hill Ryerson Ltd, 300 Water St, Whitby, Ontario L1N 9B6, Canada. Telephone: 905 430 5000. Fax: 905 430 5020.

Long renowned as the authoritative source for self-guided learning – with more than 50 million copies sold worldwide – the **teach yourself** series includes over 500 titles in the fields of languages, crafts, hobbies, business, computing and education.

British Library Cataloguing in Publication Data: a catalogue record for this title is available from The British Library.

Library of Congress Catalog Card Number: on file.

First published in UK 2008 by Hodder Education, part of Hachette Livre UK, 338 Euston Road, London NW1 3BH.

First published in US 2008 by The McGraw-Hill Companies, Inc.

The **teach yourself** name is a registered trademark of Hodder Headline.

Computer hardware and software brand names mentioned in this book are protected by their respective trademarks and are acknowledged.

Copyright © 2008 Moira Stephen

Typeset by MacDesign, Southampton

Printed in Great Britain for Hodder Education, a division of Hodder Headline, an Hachette Livre UK Company, 338 Euston Road, London NW1 3BH, by Cox & Wyman Ltd, Reading, Berkshire.

The publisher has used its best endeavours to ensure that the URLs for external websites referred to in this book are correct and active at the time of going to press. However, the publisher and the author have no responsibility for the websites and can make no guarantee that a site will remain live or that the content will remain relevant, decent or appropriate.

Hachette Livre UK's policy is to use papers that are natural, renewable and recyclable products and made from wood grown in sustainable forests. The logging and manufacturing processes are expected to conform to the environmental regulations of the country of origin.

Impression number   10 9 8 7 6 5 4 3 2

Year   2012 2011 2010 2009 2008

v

contents

preface

Teach Yourself Basic Computer Skills is for anyone who wants to learn how to make good use of their PC. It doesn't assume that you are a complete novice – there are very few of those left! You have sat at a keyboard and done a little with one application perhaps, and now want to get to grips with more. You may even be thinking of taking a basic qualification in IT. This book will get you off to a good start with Word, Excel, Access, PowerPoint, the Internet and email.

The book starts by looking at the world of ICT (Information and Communications Technology). You are introduced to the jargon, PCs in the home, education and work, legal considerations and e-commerce.

Chapter 2 goes on to help you get started using your PC and working in Windows. You will be taken from switching on, through customizing your desktop, using the online Help, managing your folders and files and installing software.

Chapter 3 covers features that are pretty standard across the Microsoft Office applications, such as creating, saving, printing, closing and opening files. Other topics include basic formatting options, moving and copying text and data, spell checking, searching, clip art and drawing.

Word is introduced in Chapter 4. You will learn how to create and manipulate basic documents, format using tabs and indents, create and edit tables, use styles and templates, perform a mail merge and create and format graphs.

In Chapter 5 you will find out how to unleash the power of Excel. As you create and format your worksheets, you will find out how to build formulas, use functions and create and format graphs.

The Access database package is introduced in Chapter 6. You will learn how to create tables and input and edit data. You will also find out how to create forms and use them for data input, manipulate your data by sorting and querying it, and present your data effectively using reports.

Chapter 7 will teach you how to create effective presentations using Microsoft PowerPoint. You will find out how to add text, tables, pictures, charts and other objects to your slides. You will also learn how to add special effects and present the finished product.

Finally, Chapter 8 introduces you to the Internet and email. You will learn how to locate websites, surf the Net, customize your browser and manage your Favorites. You will also find out how to send and reply to emails, send attachments and manage your messages.

I hope you enjoy *Teach Yourself Basic Computer Skills*, and make good use of your new skills.

Moira Stephen

2008

01

information and computer technology

In this chapter you will learn

- what ICT is about
- about computer hardware, software and information networks
- how ICT is used in everyday life
- about health and safety, environmental and security issues
- about some key legal issues
- how to tackle problems

1.1   A brief history lesson

Some of the theories and ideas that would eventually come together to help make up the modern computer were conceived back in the 19th century.

In the 1830s, Charles Babbage, an English inventor, devised a number of calculating machines. His Analytical Engine (although never actually built) was designed to perform some of the tasks a digital computer performs today, e.g. store instructions, perform calculations and have a permanent memory (punched cards would have been used). Had it been built it would have been huge – covering an area about the size of a football pitch!

In the 1840s, George Boole devised a system of mathematics which became known as Boolean Algebra. The system used binary (true/false) logic and is central to how computers make decisions.

By the end of the century, analogue computers appeared. Herman Hollerith, a US inventor, patented a calculating machine. It used punched cards and in 1890 was used to compute census data.

It was during the 20th century that the developments leading to our modern computers took place.

In the first quarter, Hollerith's Tabulating Machine Company experienced several mergers. In 1924 it was finally absorbed into a company which adopted the name International Business Machines Corporation (IBM).

World War II provided a huge stimulus to computer development. Howard Aiken, an American, led the development of a computer known as the Mark 1. It was used by the naval artillery. The British developed a computer, Colossus, that was used to decode German messages at Bletchley Park.

Shortly after the war, the Americans built the ENIAC – the most sophisticated computer of its time.

In 1947 Bell Laboratories in the USA invented the transistor. A few years later the microchip and microprocessor were invented. These developments allowed information to be stored and manipulated in a small space.

In the 1960s, index cards were still used for many data-sorting operations.

In 1974, Micro Instrumentation Telemetry Systems (MITS), in Albuquerque, New Mexico, released the Altair 8800, the first personal computer.

The next year, the Microsoft Corporation was founded by William H. Gates III (Bill Gates) and Paul Allen. They collaborated on the first version of the BASIC programming language for the MITS Altair. In 1979 they moved Microsoft to a suburb of their home town of Seattle, Washington. Two years later, Microsoft took its first step in diversifying beyond programming languages when it released MS-DOS, the operating system for the original IBM PC. Microsoft went on to convince other PC manufacturers to license MS-DOS, which made it the de facto software standard for PCs. Microsoft moved into application software, e.g. Word and Excel, and extended beyond the PC. In 1984 they began to produce application software for the Apple Macintosh.

Between 1969 and the mid-1980s, ARPAnet, a long-distance network devised by the US Government's Advanced Research Projects Agency took the first faltering steps towards what is now the Internet. From an initial network with four computers in 1969, another 200 computers in military and research establishments across the US were linked together using this network during the 1970s. By the mid-1980s several academic networks had also been set up. These combined with the ARPAnet to form the Internet. The Internet became the most exciting, fastest growing area with computer users getting hooked up at a phenomenal rate.

Computers became progressively smaller, better and cheaper in the 1980s, and by 1992, the computer industry was the fastest growing industry in the world.

1991 saw the end of a decade of collaboration between Microsoft and IBM – they went their separate ways on the next generation of operating systems for personal computers. IBM chose to pursue a former joint venture with Microsoft on the OS/2 operating system, while Microsoft chose to evolve Windows, delivering Windows 3.1 in 1992. There have been further developments of Windows since then, and by the end of the 20th century Microsoft had cornered the lion's share of the PC software market with its Windows operating system, desktop applications and Internet browser.

And today, where would we be without computers? They guide aircraft, control traffic, process words and numbers, store medical and dental records, and keep track of appointments – not to mention store photographs and play DVDs and music! You can use them to book your holidays, buy wine, do your banking or research your favourite hobby. They have become the heart of modern business, research, and indeed, everyday life.

1.2 Hardware

Computer hardware is the term used to refer to the physical parts of the computer – the bits you can see, touch, feel – and kick when things get really bad (not recommended!). The monitor, printer, keyboard, mouse, trackerball, storage devices (hard drive, memory stick), speakers, central processing unit, electronic components, boards, memory, etc. are all items of hardware.

Types of computer

Personal computer (PC)

The type of computer that you are most likely to use is the PC. Originally the PC was developed and marketed by IBM. Launched in 1981, it became a great success, so much so that other companies copied it and marketed their own PC 'clones' as IBM-compatible PCs.

The PC is a desktop computer consisting of a monitor, keyboard, mouse and a box containing the electronics, hard drive, memory, etc. The box may be under the monitor (in a desktop model), or it may be standing beside it or on the floor (a tower model).

Your home computer, or the one that you use in the office at work or in your local library is likely to be a personal computer.

Laptop (sometimes called a notebook)

As people began to rely more on their PC for business and personal use, the demand for a portable PC grew. This led to the development of laptops – smaller PCs powered by batteries that could be carried about in a briefcase. As the PCs were battery powered they would only work for a few hours before they had to be recharged – which meant you might need to take the charger with you (and perhaps a spare battery). Portable printers were designed so that you could print out your work while you were out and about, and, if you wanted to send/receive data and faxes, a cellular phone (connected to your laptop using an interface card and cable) could be used. A large (pretty large) briefcase would be needed to carry all this hardware – useful, but perhaps a less 'portable' solution than it first appears.

You often see people carrying laptops to and from work. Your children (especially student-age children!) might pester you for a laptop as it is small – so it will fit into their room easily, and they can take it with them and work on it when travelling from one place to another, or in the cafe or bar. Many laptops are WiFi enabled (see section 1.9 *Network types* below) so they can access the Internet without the need for cables.

Tablet PC

A tablet PC is a type of notebook computer that has an LCD screen that the user can write on using a stylus (or select options by touching the screen with a finger). Tablet PCs are smaller than laptops making them even more portable. They may also be more accessible for users who cannot use a keyboard although they also typically have a keyboard and/or a mouse for input.

Delivery people often have tablet PCs with them that they ask you to sign to confirm receipt of your goods.

Hand-held devices/palmtops

These PCs are small enough to be held in the palm of your hand. They use scaled down versions of desktop software. They are very popular at a professional and personal level.

The range of hand-held devices is continually expanding, with more facilities and features being added to them all the time. Terms that describe the various devices include Personal Digital Assistant (PDA), mobile phone, smart phone and multimedia player. As they become more sophisticated the technologies on each increases with the result that they are converging, so some devices are a little difficult to define.

The **Personal Digital Assistant** (PDA) is a type of hand-held computer for personal and professional use. Originally designed as electronic organizers, they have developed into powerful devices.

You can buy PDAs from many high street stores. Standard features that you would expect on a PDA are:

- Personal information management or PIM. You would expect them to be able to store contact information (names, addresses, phone numbers, email addresses), make task or to-do lists, take notes, write memos, remind you of appointments (with clock and alarm functions), plan projects, do calculations and keep track of expenses.

- Some of the more sophisticated models may be able to send or receive email, do word processing, play MP3 music files and/or MPEG movie files, access the Internet, play video games, and integrate things such as digital cameras and GPS receivers (global positioning systems used for navigation).

You can easily transfer data from your office or home PC onto your PDA, so they are very popular with people on the move, e.g. doctors, sales people, pilots, etc.

Mobile phone – the main feature on a mobile phone is the ability to make and receive calls. However, they also allow text messaging, many offer Internet access, and most have a calendar for appointments, games, and often a camera built in!

Smart phone – a sophisticated mobile phone that will run scaled down desktop software as well as offer all the features you would expect on a high-end mobile phone.

Multimedia player – a device that plays music and videos. The most famous portable device is probably the iPod – which also allows you to download your music, surf the Web with WiFi and has a host of other features.

1.3 Main parts of a computer

The main parts of a computer are the electronics, which include the central processing unit (CPU), main memory, storage devices and input and output devices.

The CPU, main memory and hard disk drive (which is one of the storage devices) are stored in the processing unit on a PC (either a desktop or tower, metal or plastic box, depending on the model). In other types, e.g. laptop or tablet, these components are stored in the main unit of the computer.

Central Processing Unit (CPU)

The CPU is often referred to as the brain of the computer. It performs the core processing, logic control and calculation work on the information which is either input by the operator or specified by the software. It controls the information flow between secondary memory and main memory. A CPU constructed on a single chip is called a microprocessor.

Types of memory

Random Access Memory (RAM) is often referred to as main memory. The programs and data you are working on are stored in RAM. RAM is volatile memory – when the computer is switched off anything in RAM is lost. The CPU controls the flow of programs and data to and from RAM. Data that has been stored on disk is transferred into RAM when you open a file to work on it.

PCs will typically have between 256Mb and 2Gb of RAM. Many new applications will not run satisfactorily on less than 256Mb. It is possible to add more RAM if you wish.

Read Only Memory (ROM) is memory that stores instructions and data that can be read, but it cannot be updated. Essential program instructions needed to start your computer up and load the operating system are stored in ROM. That is how, when you switch a computer on, it prepares itself for your use and takes you through to the screen that you start up from – the Desktop on a PC.

The CPU can read the contents of ROM, but can't add anything to it. ROM is also available on CDs and DVDs where it is sometimes referred to as secondary memory.

Hard disk drive

Most computers will usually be sold with a hard disk drive (HDD) built into them. The hard disk will contain your computer programs and your data.

You can buy additional HDDs to increase your storage space – and you can get either drives that fit inside your PC or ones that plug into your PC but sit outside the unit as a peripheral. External drives are usually more expensive than internal ones, and the cost of a drive increases with its capacity. Typically, HDDs store between 80Gb and 320Gb.

Common input devices

An input device is any device that enables you to enter text, data and instructions into your computer. The most common ones are:

Keyboard used to type information into your computer.

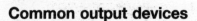

Mouse allows data input by clicking to select options (rather than typing).

Common output devices

Output devices are ones that help you get your information out of the computer in a meaningful way. The most regularly used output devices are:

Monitor or Visual Display Unit (VDU)

Information that has been entered into the computer can be viewed on the monitor.

The size of a VDU varies. The measurement quoted is for the diagonal measurement of the screen itself.

Most PCs come with a 15" or 17" VDU, with 19" monitors becoming standard on the more expensive systems. Prices are coming down and 19" and 21" VDUs are becoming more affordable.

Many PCs now have flat screens that have very high resolution e.g. 1440 × 900. These are particularly suitable when viewing DVDs, pictures, games or TV on your PC.

VDU jargon

Pixels – dots of light on the screen.

Resolution – the number of pixels on the screen. Generally speaking, the more pixels the better the picture. A resolution of 800 × 600 means that there are 800 pixels across and 600 down the screen. A resolution of 1024 × 768 is also common.

Refresh rate (or scan rate) – the frequency at which the dots of light flash on the screen. Typically, the refresh rate is 60 times per second.

Printer

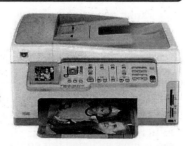

Printers are used to produce hard copy (a printout) of documents – text, graphs, pictures, etc. There are different types of printers, each with their own advantages and disadvantages.

Inkjet printers use very fine drops of ink to form the letters, etc. They are relatively slow, with speeds of 5–15 ppm (pages per minute), but the colour models give impressive results. They are good for home use, or where low volume printing is required – they are cheap to buy, but the ink cartridges are expensive.

Laser printers use heat to transfer dry toner powder onto paper. They are good for business use where high quality high volume printing is required, and can work at up to 24 ppm. These are more expensive to buy, but the running costs are lower if you do a lot of printing.

You may also come across a **dot matrix printer** – an older, noisier type of printer, used where carbon copies are required.

With any type of printer, specifications and costs vary greatly. Some print in black and white only, others print in colour – and this affects the price, running costs and speed. If you are looking to buy a printer, check out the Web or your local computer shop.

Computer ports

Your input and output devices are connected to your computer using a port – the interface that connects one computer device to another. The most common are USB, serial, parallel, FireWire and network port.

Serial ports send one bit of data at a time between the devices.

Parallel ports send several bits of data between devices at a time.

The **USB** port has become the most common type in recent years. It can connect a wide range of peripherals to your PC, e.g. mouse, keyboard, PDAs, gamepad, joystick, scanner, digital cameras, printers, personal media player, and USB pens/flash drives.

FireWire is Apple Inc.'s brand name for the IEEE 1394 interface. It gives a high-speed data transfer that will accommodate multimedia applications. Most digital camcorders have included this connection since 1995 and computers for professional or home audio/video use tend to have built-in FireWire ports.

A **network** port uses numbers to identify different types of ports on the network, e.g. port 80 is used for http traffic.

1.4 PC performance

A number of factors can affect a computer's performance – the speed at which it performs the tasks requested of it. You can judge a computer's performance in a number of ways – perhaps the amount of time it takes to open an application or file, or the amount of time it takes to display a graphic on the screen. Things that may affect the performance are:

• The **clock speed** of the CPU. This is the speed at which it can process information. It is measured in megahertz (MHz) or gigahertz (GHz). Mega = million, Giga = billion, Hertz = cycles per second. A clock speed of 600 MHz therefore means that the processor can operate at 600 million cycles per second.

The clock speed of a computer is one of the factors that can influence its performance. Generally speaking, the higher the clock speed the more expensive the computer. Intel and AMD are the main producers and suppliers of microprocessors.

• The **amount of RAM**.

• The type and **speed of the graphics processor** in the computer.

• The **size of the HDD**.

• The **access speed of the HDD**. The time taken for the unit to search for, identify and process data saved on the disk is measured in milliseconds (msec). In general, larger capacity HDDs tend to have a faster access time than smaller ones.

• The **access speed of any peripheral device** that the computer gets information from, e.g. modem, external drives.

• The **number of applications running** at the same time. The more applications that you run simultaneously, the more computer memory and processing power you require.

For a PC to operate at its optimum level, the capability of the components used in the system must be balanced. There is little point having 750 Mb of RAM and a 400 Gb HDD on a computer with a 133 MHz chip – the processor speed would not allow the optimum performance of the memory or HDD.

1.5 Units of measurement

The unit of measurement used to describe the storage capacities of memory and disks on computers are bits, bytes, kilobytes, megabytes and gigabytes.

As storage capacity is constantly increasing, the measurements most often used are kilobytes (Kb), megabytes (Mb), gigabytes (Gb) and terabyes (Tb).

1 bit: The amount of storage space needed to hold either a 1 or 0 in memory. Bit = Binary digit.

1 byte: Is equal to 8 bits. Every character, e.g. 'a', '2', 'z', '?', 'm', is made up of 8 bits (one byte), so each takes up one byte of storage space.

1 kilobyte (Kb): 1024 bytes. That's about enough to store the text of this section, or about half a page of A4.

1 megabyte (Mb): 1024 Kb, about 1 million bytes. Memory size is usually quoted in Mb – typically a PC will have between 256 and 750 Mb of memory (although more can be added). High density diskettes, the standard floppy disks, have a capacity of 1.44 Mb – not a lot of storage if you are storing music, photographs or video.

1 gigabyte (Gb): 1024 Mb, about 1 billion bytes. Hard disk sizes are usually quoted in Gb – on new PCs this will typically be about 80 Gb or more.

1 terabyte (Tb): 1024 Gb, about 1 trillion bytes. A lot of storage!

1.6 Storage media

Hard Disk Drives (HDDs): Discussed above.

Network drive: A drive on a computer network. It may be an actual drive, or a *logical* drive – a section of a physical drive.

Compact disk (CD or CD-ROM): These have been used on PCs for several years. They are ideally suited for storing information that doesn't need updating often, e.g. application packages (you buy the next version if you want to change it), encyclopaedias, e.g. Encarta, clip art, etc. In addition to storage capacity, increased speed of access is another benefit of CDs.

You can also get CDs that you can write to, in the same way as to a HDD. There are two types of these: CD-R (Recordable) and CD-RW (ReWriteable). With a CD-R you can use the disk to record information once only – once you've recorded something on it you can't re-record. With a CD-RW you can record, and re-record, as often as you want – the disks are reusable. Both have a capacity of 650–750 Mb.

Digital Versatile Disks (DVDs): DVDs are also popular. You can store audio, video or computer program data on a DVD. CD-ROMs can be used in a DVD drive, but a DVD disk will not operate in a CD drive. DVD-R (recordable) is also available. They can hold 4–5 Gb of data.

USB flash drive: A small, lightweight, removable, rewriteable storage device integrated with a USB connector so you can plug it into your computer. They are about the size of a small highlighter pen. Their storage capacity varies considerably from 128 Mb up to several Gb.

Memory card: A memory or flash memory card is a storage device used with digital cameras, hand-held and mobile computers, telephones, music players, video game consoles, etc. They offer high re-recordability, power-free storage, small format and rugged specifications.

Online file storage: Sometimes referred to as a file hosting service or online media centre. The service is specifically designed to host static content, typically large files that are not web pages.

The storage devices discussed above are sometimes referred to as secondary storage.

1.7 Peripherals

Any piece of equipment attached to a PC rather than built into it is called a peripheral device. Printers, scanners, external drives, external modems, speakers, amplifiers, etc. are all peripheral devices. Peripherals can enhance the capabilities of your PC.

Input

The most common input devices, keyboard and mouse, were discussed earlier. Other input devices include:

Trackerball and touchpad

These are often found on laptops instead of a mouse. A trackerball is like an upside down mouse, and you use your fingertips to move the ball (which has the effect of moving the mouse pointer on the screen). A touchpad senses a fingertip being drawn across it and moves the mouse pointer on the screen accordingly.

Scanner

Scanners are used to convert printed material into a digitized form that can be imported into an application package. The scanner will take a picture of the printed material, and this can then be stored or viewed on your PC. If you wish to scan in text then edit it in a word processor, the scanner will need Optical Character Recognition (OCR) software to convert the printed image into text.

* You will also find combined printers and scanners for sale – these can be useful for home use where they are not heavily used and space is at a premium.

Graphics tablet

This is a touch-sensitive pad that has a stylus attached to it. The stylus can be used to write or draw freehand onto the pad, and the data is converted into a digitized form that can be used in your computer.

Digital camera

Images are stored in a digital format in the camera, directly onto magnetic media. They can then be downloaded into your PC, and edited/printed and stored as required.

Voice recognition

A microphone is attached to a PC that has appropriate voice recognition software on it. When you speak into the microphone the speech is converted into text. The text can then be stored, edited and printed as required. This method of input could be very useful for visually or physically impaired PC users.

Joystick

A hand-held device that swivels in its socket so you can move around the screen. It will have buttons and triggers on it so you can click on things and 'shoot' things – typically used when playing games.

Webcam

A device used to take video and transmit it over the Web.

Microphone

A device for recording audio onto your computer – you could use one to record a narrative for some pictures in a presentation.

Stylus

An input device often used with a PDA or touch screen. It looks like a ballpoint pen.

Output devices

An output device is any device that allows what is on your PC to be seen or heard. Output devices that you are likely to be most familiar with are the monitor and a printer (discussed above).

Other output devices that you may meet include:

Plotters

These are a specialized type of printer used in design environments for things like technical drawings or architectural plans. They can print out large, complex hard copies. The software controls a type of pen that moves in two dimensions over paper.

Speakers

These tend to come as standard on a multimedia PC, the type often purchased for home use. They work in the same way as speakers attached to stereo equipment. Speakers on a PC may be self-powered, with a small amplifier built in. They usually need a soundcard to be fitted inside the computer and the speakers are then connected to this. You may also find the speakers built into the monitor.

Headphones

These allow you to hear output from your computer without disturbing anyone else.

Speech synthesizer software translates written text into audible speech. It has specialist uses, e.g. to help people with impaired vision or those with physical disabilities.

Input/output devices

Some devices can be used for both input and output, e.g. touch screens. They are output in that they are screens, like VDUs that display data from your computer, and they are input in that you can select options and give instructions by touching the appropriate bit of the screen.

1.8 Software

Software refers to the programs that make your computer work. These includes the operating system (essential to get your computer up and running) and the applications, e.g. software that lets you carry out specific tasks (word processing, spreadsheets, email, database, etc.).

Operating systems (OS)

The operating system performs a range of basic tasks, such as recognizing input from the keyboard, sending output to the screen, keeping track of files and folders on the disk, and controlling peripheral devices such as disk drives and printers.

The operating system provides a software platform on top of which application programs can run. It is essential to the efficient running of the PC. It controls which operations within the computer are carried out and in what order they are done.

When a computer is switched on it is said to *boot-up*. During the boot-up process it carries out a Power On Self Test (POST) to check that the hardware components are present and working properly and to check that the CPU and memory are functioning correctly. The next thing that the computer does when it boots-up is to locate and load the OS (or part of the OS). The OS is usually stored on disk, e.g. in your *Windows* folder. The OS is loaded into RAM at this stage.

The OS that you will become familiar with when working through this book is Microsoft Windows Vista. Previous versions of Windows include 98, 2000, Me (Millennium Edition), NT and XP. Each of these is a different version of Windows and Windows 98 is the oldest of these. As software develops and new or better features are added, the software company releases a new version of the software, and identifies it by changing the name slightly. A new version of Windows is released approximately every 18 months to 2 years. If you can use one version, you will very quickly learn how to use any other.

Windows has a Graphical User Interface (GUI) – it uses pictures (icons) to show the facilities available on the PC rather than words. You can select a feature by pointing to it with the mouse and then clicking on the feature you want to choose. Using a GUI as the front end to an OS makes it much easier for a user to tell the system what to do. Apple Macs also have a GUI.

Application packages

Computer programs such as word processing, spreadsheet, database, etc. are called application packages. These are separate from the OS, but must be compatible with it. If you read the information on the box of an application package in a computer store, it will tell you what OS it is compatible with.

As with operating system software, new versions of the main application packages are released about every 18 months to 2 years. The most recent version of office is Office 2007. You may find yourself using Microsoft Office 95, or 97, 2000, XP or 2003. Each new version improves on the last (usually), or introduces something new, but the core functions and features have remained constant for many years. The look of Office 2007 is, however, quite different from earlier versions.

Popular application packages are:

Email – used to send electronic mail messages across the Internet and over computer networks. Once you have your email system set up it is a very quick way of sending messages. The messages could just be short text messages, or you can attach files, photographs and include links to websites. We will introduce Outlook, the Microsoft email program in Chapter 8.

Web-browsing – popular applications include Internet Explorer, Netscape Navigator, Firefox, Safari and Mozilla.

Photo-editing – to allow you to work with the photographs you have taken on your digital camera. You can remove red-eye, improve the contrast, crop the edges, etc.

Word processing – used to produce reports, memos, letters, books – anything that is text based.

Spreadsheet – you can enter text and numbers into a spreadsheet, and, more importantly, perform calculations on the numbers and produce graphs.

Database – used to keep data on customers, suppliers, stock items, library books, etc. Data from a database can be extracted using different criteria, e.g. you might want a list of all the books in your library by a particular author.

Presentation – allows the creation of sophisticated presentations with text, pictures, graphs, animation effects, video and music.

Desktop Publishing (DTP) – used for newsletters, posters, invitations, etc. where you want to have a lot of control over where you place your text and graphics on a page. Many of the more sophisticated word processing packages have similar capabilities to a DTP package.

Graphic design – giving designers the opportunity to produce complex, detailed designs that can be edited and updated quickly and easily.

Accounts – used by companies to keep track of their cash flow.

Games – loads are available, there's something to suit every age group.

Many applications packages are sold as a suite, e.g. Microsoft Office or Microsoft Works. The suites contain a set of packages, e.g. word processing, spreadsheet, presentation, database, desk top publishing. Both Office and Works are popular suites found in the home and in all types of businesses. The applications in Office are much more powerful and sophisticated than those in Works making it more suited to business use.

Accessibility features

Many of today's software applications have features that improve the accessibility of the software for all users. Accessibility features include:

* Voice recognition for input.

* Screen reader that reads what is on the screen for people that can't see the text clearly.

* Screen magnifiers.

* On-screen keyboard to ease input of text and data.

1.9 Network types

You can use your PC as a stand-alone computer, or you can link it together with other computers to form a network. A network may consist of a couple of computers in the same office sharing a printer and files – or thousands of computers connected across the globe.

Local Area Network (LAN)

A LAN is made up of computers connected together by cables or wireless in the same room or building. The computers are in close proximity (local) to each other.

PCs can be networked in a peer-to-peer setup that allows peripherals, e.g. printers and scanners to be shared. A user can also access files on another user's hard drive in this type of network.

Alternatively, PCs can be networked through a central computer (called a server or file server) where they can share drives and folders. These are called client–server networks. Each user is allocated an area of hard drive on the file server for their own data files. The server also stores main application software that can be run over the whole network, e.g. email, anti-virus, etc. Backup procedures are simplified for users as all files on the file server can be backed up at the same time (often at night, when most people have stopped work and gone home) rather than each user having to back up the files from their own PC.

File servers are intended for business rather than personal use and they are more expensive than standard PCs.

Benefits of linking PCs together into a LAN are that several PCs can share the same peripherals, applications and data files, and can communicate using email (if email software is installed).

Wireless Local Area Network (WLAN)

There has been a rise in wireless network computing in the past few years. Initially pretty much confined to academic circles (i.e. university campuses), health-care, manufacturing, and warehousing, it is now becoming available to the general public. The number of *hotspots* in airport lounges, coffee shops, etc. is increasing.

A **hotspot** is a location where high-speed Internet access is available to any WiFi-enabled computer, thanks to a WLAN access point. Many handheld and laptop computers and PDAs are now WiFi-enabled. Access coverage extends up to a 300-foot radius depending on location and equipment.

WiFi – a standard that allows your PC to access a WLAN, which in turn may allow access to the Internet and your email.

Wide Area Network (WAN)

Computers connected over a long distance are part of a WAN. Large organizations may use a WAN to connect their offices in different parts of the country. For example, an organization with branches in London, Cardiff, Leeds, Birmingham, Glasgow and Edinburgh may have the offices connected using a WAN (the computers within each branch would be connected using a LAN). The WAN could use leased lines (perhaps from BT or Mercury) for the exclusive use of the organization.

The advantages of linking PCs to a WAN is that data can be transferred a long distance very quickly (e.g. from your London office to your office in Edinburgh).

A computer linked to another via a modem over the telephone line would be part of a WAN. Computers linked via the Internet form a WAN. A PC attached to a WAN can have access to huge amounts of information (on the Internet) and communicate with others using email (which is much quicker than sending information using the traditional mail service).

Internet

The Internet is a huge WAN, linking computers from all over the world. To access the Internet you need:

- A computer linked to the telephone network via a modem (if you're linked to an analogue line) or a computer linked to the ISDN network using an ISDN adapter.

- Internet access software.

- Browser software, e.g. Internet Explorer or Netscape Navigator, to look at web pages and explore the Web.

- An account with an Internet Service Provider (ISP). Your ISP will provide you with a connection to the Internet. You may be charged by the minute, usually at the same rate as a local phone call, or pay a fixed monthly fee for unlimited access.

You can access the World Wide Web via the Internet, send emails, access your company computer system and transfer files, etc.

The Internet is also used as a collaborative tool where groups of people that are remote from each other can share information, research findings, etc. New ways of communicating have evolved, e.g. web logs (blogs), forums and discussion groups, social networks like Bebo and Facebook and instant messaging e.g. MSN.

Intranet

The intranet is a private network that uses Internet features to give insiders access to company data. A company intranet looks and feels like the Internet to its users, but the pages are internal to the organization. The information is displayed on web style pages, and *hyperlinks* (addresses attached to text or images) let users jump from place to place, but the data will be held on a company server, with access limited to company employees.

From the company's point of view, an intranet has three attractive features often missing when it comes to Internet use:

* Speed.
* Security (it is a private internal network – LAN or WAN – protected from Internet users by a firewall (special security hardware and/or software).
* Control (it is managed by your own staff).

Extranet

An extranet is a private network that uses the Internet technology and the public telecommunication system to securely share part of a business's information or operations with suppliers, customers, or other businesses. An extranet can be viewed as part of a company's intranet that is extended to users outside the company. Users can log into the extranet over the Internet by entering their username and password.

Transferring data

Downloading and uploading files

When working with networks you will hear the terms downloading and uploading used. This simply means transferring data between computers on a network. You download a file from the server to your own computer. You upload a file from your own computer to the server.

Transfer rates

The transfer rate is the speed at which data is transferred across the network (also known as the baud rate). It can vary from fairly slow, e.g. 14,400 bps (bits per second) up to 56,600 bps on modems and dial-up lines. Broadband connections and faster devices may have the transfer rate quoted in kilobits per second (kbps) or megabits per second (mbps).

Connecting to the Internet

When connecting to the Internet you might use a dial-up service (where you dial up each time you want a connection). With a dial-up service you are charged according to how much use you make of the service – just like using your normal telephone.

You can also connect to the Internet using a mobile phone, via cable, wireless or satellite.

Many people have a broadband connection to the Internet. Broadband has the advantage of always being on and available for use (unless there is a technical problem). It is usually charged at a flat rate per month (no matter how much use you make of it) and it is high speed.

It is also relatively easy for intruders to access your broadband connection unless you take steps to avoid this happening.

1.10 Information technology and ICT

Information technology refers to any means of storing, processing and transmitting information using modern technology. The term *Information and Communication Technology* (ICT) also encompasses facsimile, telephone, multimedia presentations, etc. as well as computers.

e-commerce

The Internet has facilitated the expansion of e-commerce. Companies can advertise their products on their own websites, take orders, and accept payment via secure credit card transfer.

Many goods bought over the Internet are cheaper than they would be in the high street, as the company doesn't have the overhead of a shop front in a prime location. However, you have to decide what you want without actually seeing it (all you have is a picture on your screen), and this can be a disadvantage (unless you have already seen the product elsewhere).

There are obvious security issues when it comes to e-commerce. You must give your name and delivery address so that your purchases can be forwarded to you. You must also provide credit card information so that you can pay for the goods. Legitimate companies that conduct their transactions electronically take steps to ensure that their sites are secure and the information that you provide is safe.

As with all remote shopping, try to ensure that you do business with reputable companies. If a deal sounds too good to be true and the company is one that you haven't heard of, you would be wise to be wary.

e-government

e-government refers to the government's use of ICT to exchange information and services with citizens, businesses and other arms of government.

It may be applied to the process of developing legislation, the work of the legal systems in the courts, or the administration in government departments with a view to improving internal efficiency or the delivery of public services. The most important anticipated benefits of e-government include improved efficiency, convenience, and better accessibility of public services.

e-banking

e-banking is an umbrella term for the banking transactions and activities that you can perform electronically – without visiting your bank. It is also called Internet banking, online banking, and home banking – the terms are used interchangeably.

You can usually check your bank balance, transfer funds from one account to another, pay bills, etc.

Almost anything you can do at a normal bank can be done on line – with the exception of extracting cash from your machine!

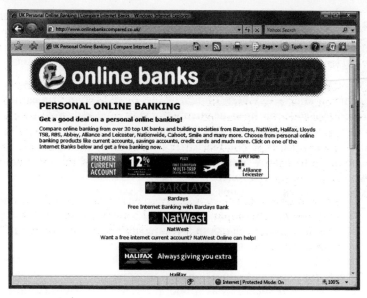

e-learning

Many courses can also be studied over the Internet. This is referred to as e-learning and if you have been studying recently you will probably have used a virtual learning environment. Your notes and exercises will be available to you via the Internet, you will be able to contact your tutor via email, and you may be able to take part in discussion groups and forums with others studying the same course.

e-learning in its various forms is a popular learning tool. Learning materials can be made much more exciting with the use of multimedia – audio, video, graphics, animations, text, etc. The materials can be made interactive, and simulation packages may allow the learner to experience the situation.

Communication through virtual learning environments, blogs, podcasts, forums and discussion groups can be used to encourage participation and ensure that the learner remains focused.

The learning materials can be accessed at a time that is convenient to the learner, so students can use the environment to learn at their own pace, and go back through material that they haven't quite grasped. Computerized exercises and games can be used to help reinforce the learning process. Sophisticated Computer Based Training (CBT) packages are available for all ages and situations – they may be used to help toddlers to count, or medical students learn about the body or pilots how to fly aeroplanes.

Companies find e-learning a cost-effective way to train staff. Once a course has been bought it can be used many times for different staff (or the same member of staff over and over again). A possible disadvantage of e-learning is that you might not have access to a tutor to ask when you don't understand something, and you may be working on your own, so you can't compare notes or discuss problems with your peers. This is less of an issue if discussion groups and virtual classrooms are utilized.

In addition to e-learning, educational establishments also use applications in the classroom that are similar to those found in industry, e.g. the Microsoft Works suite to familiarize pupils with the type of software they will meet later in life. The administration requirements of educational establishments mean that typical business applications as found in the Microsoft Office suite are usually required, e.g. database for student/pupil records, word processing for minutes, reports, teaching materials, etc.

Home working/teleworking

The number of people working from home has increased as many jobs that traditionally had to be done in the office can be carried out successfully on a home PC with Internet access.

Home working is also referred to as teleworking and the term SoHo (small office/home office) may also be used when discussing home working.

The benefits of home working are that:

- It is flexible (you don't need to stick to the 9 to 5 routine).

- You don't need to join the commuter trail to and from the office each day.

- You don't get all the distractions of working in an office, e.g. your work flow broken so you can attend a meeting or deal with some crisis that has cropped up.

- You can adopt a flexible schedule to fit around your other commitments.

- Your company can save money in office space as few workers are in at any one time.

However, some teleworkers feel isolated as they miss the social interaction of a central office, and it may be difficult to feel part of a team when working remotely.

Communication

Electronic mail (email)

If you have access to the Internet you can send email to anyone else that is connected. An email is a message that is sent over a LAN or WAN. You can send text, data, pictures, etc. Messages received can be read, replied to, forwarded to someone else, stored, printed or deleted as required. Everyone that uses email has a unique address. Email is very quick and cheap and compares very favourably with the traditional mail service.

One of the main advantages of email is that it is time independent – you can send a message when it suits you, and the recipient can access it in their mailbox at a time that suits them (so it is very useful when working across time zones).

Instant Messaging (IM)

Instant messaging allows you to communicate with friends and colleagues in real time. When you access an IM system you can tell which of your contacts are online as they will be listed as logged in to the system. You have probably heard of some IM systems, e.g. MSN, Yahoo!, Google Talk. They are low cost, and allow you to transfer files as well as messages.

Voice over Internet Protocol (VoIP)

Voice over Internet Protocol (VoIP) is a protocol for transmitting voice over the Internet. VoIP is also known as IP telephony, Internet telephony, broadband telephony and voice over broadband. As an increasing number of people have broadband in their homes, there is a potential benefit in cost savings if VoIP is used on your broadband connection as you can use a single network to carry voice and data. Many home users will underutilize the network capacity of their broadband connection so VoIP means that you can also have your telephone calls at no additional cost.

Really Simple Syndication (RSS)

These are web feed formats used to publish frequently updated content, e.g. blog entries, news headlines or podcasts. RSS documents – called 'feed', 'web feed' or 'channel' – contain either a summary of content from an associated website or the full text. RSS allows people to keep up to date with what is happening on their favourite websites without checking them manually.

Blog (Weblog)

A blog is an online document where individuals or groups can publish information about themselves or some project/topic they are working on. The blog is like a journal, where the information is displayed in chronological order – the oldest entry is at the end of the blog. You can keep up to date with what is happening by reading the blog and perhaps comment on its content.

Podcast

A podcast is a digital media file (or a related collection of such files) which is distributed over the Internet to portable media players and PCs using syndication feeds. The word 'podcast' is a fusion of iPod and broadcast as the Apple iPod was the first device that used this technology. You can subscribe to podcasts so that you receive new content from them automatically when it is published. Podcasts are often distributed through RSS.

Virtual communities

An online (virtual) community is one that you may join for a variety of reasons – social, study, research, etc. Social networking sites, e.g. Facebook and Bebo have become very popular with friends and families that are geographically separate but want to keep up to date with each other regularly. You can publish your photographs, audio and video clips and information on what you have been doing on these sites. You can then give your friends and family access to your site so that they can keep up to date with what is going on in your life.

Internet forums allow you to discuss topics of interest with colleagues and peers from around the globe. You can drop into chat rooms to catch up on the gossip with your friends and play online computer games with people you may never meet. Sites like Second Life give you the chance to become a member of a virtual community where you have your own fictitious character and role in life.

See Chapter 8 for additional information on these services, the potential risks that they may carry and how to avoid those risks.

Safety first

Being able to communicate with your friends and family so easily over the Internet is great! And social networking sites are a great way to keep in touch with friends and make new friends with people from all over the world that share your interests. But be careful!! If you meet someone new on these sites you have no real way of knowing who they are, so keep a few common-sense precautions in mind:

DO NOT make your profile public – keep it private.

DO NOT post personal information about yourself – your address, phone number, email address.

Remember that the information that you post is publicly available – and be very wary of strangers!

1.11 Looking after yourself

A good workspace

It is important that your work area is comfortable and suitable for the type of work you are doing. It must conform to the relevant Health and Safety at Work (HASAW) legislation.

Ergonomics is all about ensuring that your work area is safe and comfortable for you to work in. It is about making sure that the layout of your work area does not adversely affect your well-being. An ergonomically well designed workspace will ensure that the computer operator is comfortable when working.

Things to consider when assessing whether or not the working environment is suitable for computer use include:

Lighting and ventilation

- Provision of adequate lighting and ventilation.
- Positioning of VDUs – the screens should not flicker or suffer from interference, and they should be free from glare.
- Provision of blinds if necessary to minimize the effect of direct sunlight on the VDU.

Operator comfort

- Suitable desktop space.
- There should be sufficient desk room and leg room to allow for posture changes.
- An adjustable chair.
- Provision of movable keyboards.
- Provision of a document holder at a suitable height.
- Minimized printer noise (this was a particular problem with dot matrix printers).
- Operators should take regular 'stretching' breaks from their computer.
- Eye relaxation techniques may help.

Safety

- No trailing cables or power leads.

- No worn out or frayed power leads.
- No overloaded power points.
- No liquid near electrical components.

Health problems

Problems that may be experienced by IT workers include:

- Backache and pains in general associated with bad posture and sitting in the same position for too long.
- Repetitive Strain Injury (RSI) – the result of poor ergonomics combined with repeated movements of the same joints over a long period of time.
- Eye strain – caused by flickering VDUs and not taking breaks from the screen (10 minutes every hour is recommended).
- Back injuries due to lifting heavy objects, e.g. boxes of paper.
- Electric shocks due to dangerous wiring or incorrect working practice.
- Injuries resulting from tripping over trailing cables or other obstructions.

It is the employer's responsibility to ensure that appropriate provision is made available to provide a safe and comfortable working environment, but employees have a responsibility to ensure that they make use of them and go about their job in an appropriate manner.

The Internet is a useful resource when it comes to keeping up to date with health and safety laws and guidelines that affect the use of IT. You will find a wealth of information at:

http://www.hse.gov.uk.

The main pieces of UK legislation affecting the use of IT in the workplace are the:

- Health and Safety at Work Act (1974)
- Health and Safety (Display Screen Equipment) Regulations 1992
- Workplace (Health, Safety and Welfare) Regulations 1992
- Control of Substances Hazardous to Health (COSHH).

Environmental considerations

Computers can go through a considerable amount of consumables, e.g. printer cartridges and paper. There are recycling options for these – cartridges can be refilled, and printouts that are not required can be recycled.

With many computers being networked, it is possible to store documents on a shared drive where people can view them on the screen rather than take a printout.

There are also a number of energy-saving options that should be considered for when a computer is not in use. The monitor can be set so that it turns off automatically after a period of inactivity; the computer can be put to sleep when you are finished with it for a while; and it should be switched off at the end of the day.

1.12 Password protection

When working in a networked environment you will use a user ID and a password to access the system. These are used to identify you so that appropriate rights are made available to you while you work. These rights give you access to the drives that you need to use to read and/or write to files.

There are various levels of password protection available to help ensure that authorized users only can access the system and open and edit the files held on it.

User-level

Password protection can be assigned at a user level (through the operating system) so that only authorized users can access the system. With this type of password protection, the computer will pause as it boots up and you need to enter your user identification and password before you can go any further.

Careful consideration should be given to the passwords that you use to ensure that they cannot be guessed easily.

* Don't use things someone can associate with you (e.g. your name or your child's), your date of birth or car registration.

* Use a mixture of letters and numbers that you can remember but that you think it will be difficult for someone to guess.

* Don't tell anyone your password – and change it regularly.

* Many systems have a minimum length, e.g. 8 characters.

Folders/directories

Some folders on the file server will be shared – several users may have access to them. To ensure that authorized users only access these folders, passwords may be used.

Files

If you have files on any PC (not just on a network) that you don't want other users to be able to view or edit, you may be able to password-protect them (most modern applications allow the user to password-protect individual files).

By using the password-protection features available, the following security features could be available on a networked PC:

* A password to access the system.

* A password to access a shared folder on the network server.

* A password to access a file.

* A password to allow editing of a file.

Different users can have different levels of security clearance assigned to them, allowing different users access to different parts of the system and its files.

USB/flash drives

You can also protect the contents of some memory sticks by assigning a password to them. The contents can only be viewed if you supply the correct password.

Screen savers

Screen savers were originally designed to prevent the VDU from becoming damaged as a result of a static image being displayed on it for a long period of time. New screens do not get damaged in this way as easily as earlier models did, so screen savers are really an optional personalization feature that you can use. If you use a screen saver on your PC, you can enter a password as one of the screen saver options. When a password is set, you will have to enter the password to cancel the screen saver.

1.13 Hardware and software security

Increased use and reliance on computers has resulted in a need for users to be aware of threats to the security of equipment and information. It is also vitally important that users take appropriate steps to reduce the danger from these threats.

Your computer equipment and the data on it is a very important resource. It is therefore important that you look after it and take precautions to ensure that, should anything happen to it, you can recover from the situation.

Hardware can be protected through insurance policies – if your PC is stolen or damaged you can take precautions to ensure that you will be able to replace it. You can help minimize the risks to your hardware by ensuring that you lock your office/room and close the windows when you leave. Security cables can also be used to lock your computer and hardware down – this not only deters thieves from running off with your hardware, but it will help keep your data safe too.

Your software will probably have been installed from CD, and if it becomes corrupted you should be able to re-install it from your original disks (you should make sure that these are kept in a safe place).

However, protecting your data needs a bit more thought. Threats to your data include:

- Power cuts (where any unsaved data will be lost).
- Serious hardware fault.
- Physical damage (perhaps as a result of flood or fire).
- Infection by a computer virus.
- Theft or other malicious act.

Lost files on a home computer may cause some inconvenience, but on a business machine the effect of losing data could ruin an organization.

To minimize the effect of such incidents, you should back up the data on your HDD regularly. You may just back up important files to a flash drive, CD-R or CD-RW, or you may back up the whole drive to a DVD or external hard drive.

In a business, backups may be done every few hours, or at the end of each day, week, etc. – it depends on the organization and how much the files change in a period of time. In many organizations data is backed up overnight when most people aren't at work and the process is usually at least partially automated.

The set of media containing the backups is called the backing store. Ideally, the store should be kept offsite – at a different location to the computer that the original data is on – or at least in a different room and ideally in a different building altogether.

All backup media should be kept in an environment that is thief proof and flood and fire proof. A safe or vault is often used. Ideally more than one set of backup media should be kept.

The storage devices for backing up need to be large enough to hold all the files that are considered crucial to the operation of the organization. Specialized devices such as tape-streaming machines can be used, or CD-R or multi-gigabyte HDDs may be used.

For a home PC user, a flash drive, CD-R or CD-RW can be used for backing up your data. Exactly how often you back up will vary from individual to individual – but if you've just spent hours working on a project on your PC, it's a good idea to back up the files before you finish work.

To help protect your data from intruders on the Internet you should install a *firewall* which acts as a barrier between your computer and the Internet.

1.14 Computer viruses

A computer virus is software that has been written with the specific purpose of causing havoc on computer systems. It is called a virus because it has been programmed to spread through the system and on to other computer systems, just like an infectious virus spreads through the general population.

Some viruses may be harmless; they do no serious damage to your system, but serve to remind you just how vulnerable your system may be. Other viruses can have disastrous effects, deleting files, corrupting disks, etc.

No computer is immune from virus attack (although there aren't too many mainframe viruses), but some basic safety precautions can help limit the chances of infection:

◆ Install reliable anti-virus software on your computer, and update it regularly.

◆ Use the anti-virus software to scan your system for viruses regularly.

◆ Use the anti-virus software to scan any removable disks before you open files on them.

◆ Scan any files downloaded from the Internet before you open them – viruses are often transmitted in attachments to emails.

◆ Install only genuine software from reputable sources.

◆ Don't open attachments to emails, or the email messages themselves, from sources that you don't recognize.

The writers of viruses are always producing new threats, so it is very important that you keep your anti-virus software up to date.

When you run your anti-virus software, it will disinfect any files with a virus it recognizes. If it cannot disinfect the file, it may 'quarantine' it, or delete it to safeguard your machine.

For additional information on viruses see Chapter 8.

1.15 Legal issues

There are also a number of legal issues that computer users should be aware of.

Copyright ©

Software copyright legislation is in place to give the authors and developers of software the same rights as authors of published written or musical works.

When you buy software, you don't actually purchase the package, just a licence that allows you to use the software. The terms of the licence are known as the End User Licence Agreement. Each licence that you purchase has an identification code – you can usually check the product ID in the product information screen (Help menu > About ...).

With some licences you are permitted to install a copy of the software on one computer, and take a backup copy of it for security purposes. With other licences you may be able to install two copies of the software, e.g. one on your office machine and one on your laptop or home PC. This option recognizes the fact that people often use the software in two locations. Instead of having to buy two copies of the software you can install it on two computers – but you should only be using one copy at a time (you can't be in two places at once).

In a business situation, where you perhaps have 50 users on a network, you can buy a software licence that allows you to run the number of copies you require at any one time. This usually works out much cheaper than buying the same number of individual licences. The licence should cover the maximum number of users you expect to be using the software at any one time.

Copyright also applies to text, pictures, videos and music that you find on the Internet. If you download any of these items from the Internet with the intention of using them in your own work you should get permission from the copyright holder if at all possible. At the very least you should acknowledge your source.

Shareware

Shareware software is sold on a kind of sale-or-return basis. You can obtain the software free, use it for a limited period e.g. 30 days, then, if you decide that you want to continue to use the software you should forward that appropriate fee (typically £10 to £30) and become a registered user. At the end of the evaluation period the software may have been programmed to stop working or it may flash up messages telling you to pay up!

Sometimes the evaluation copy of a shareware package will be a scaled down version of the whole package. If you decide to pay up and register then the full package will be sent to you.

Freeware

Freeware authors and developers often produce the software to solve a particular problem they have had, or just as a personal project/challenge. Once the software is written, they make it freely available to anyone else who thinks that they'll find it useful.

If you use shareware or freeware software try to ensure that it comes from a reputable source or is recommended in PC magazines, etc. The software may not have been tested as thoroughly as commercial software and it may contain bugs or viruses. There is, however, some very good, useful and safe shareware and freeware software available – just be careful!

Open source

With open-source software, the human-readable source code is made available under a copyright licence. Users are permitted to use, change, and improve the software, and to redistribute it in modified or unmodified form. It is often developed in a public, collaborative manner. OpenOffice from Sun Microsystems is an example of a suite of office software (very similar to Microsoft Office – but much cheaper) based on open-source software

Data Protection Act

The Data Protection Act appeared in 1984 in the UK, and it was updated in 1998. It states that users of personal data relating to living, identifiable individuals which is automatically processed should be registered with the Data Protection Registrar.

The users of the personal data should then adhere to The Codes of Practice and Data Protection Principles set out within the Act.

The Data Protection Principles

The rules that must be followed by all organizations keeping personal data on individuals are listed here.

The data must be:

* Obtained lawfully.
* Held securely.
* Used only for the purpose stated to the Data Protection Registrar (or compatible purposes).
* Adequate, relevant and not excessive in relation to the purpose for which it is held.
* Accurate and kept up to date.
* Deleted when it is no longer required.
* Available to individuals so that they can access and check the information that is held on them.

As most organizations hold personal data – on their customers, employees, suppliers, patients, etc. – most (even small ones) must be registered with the Data Protection Registrar.

1.16   System maintenance

As computers are such an integral part of our lives, you should be able to do at least a little basic system maintenance. Even if you are not confident trying to fix things for yourself, knowing what to check and what to look for can be useful when discussing any problems you encounter.

Components not working

If your computer doesn't seem to be working, the first things to check are:

- **Power** – make sure that the plugs are in the sockets and that they are switched on. If that looks OK, check that the sockets are working properly – test something else in them, e.g. plug in your hairdryer or a lamp to check that it works. If the sockets are working, it might be that the plug has fused. You could change the fuse and see if that works.

- **Connections** – make sure that all the cables are connected properly. The mouse, keyboard, screen and printer should be attached to the computer's system box.

- **Hardware switched on** – many computers have switches on the actual monitor and printer – so if they don't seem to be working, check that they are actually switched on.

Error indicators

Your computer will give you clues when something is wrong. These include:

- Flashing lights, e.g. on a printer to indicate a paper jam.

- Nothing appearing on the monitor – indicating that it is switched off, or the screen saver has kicked in, or there is some other problem.

- Bleeps – when you ask your PC to perform some task that it can't do.

- No printer output – if there is no paper, or the printer is switched off.

- No pointer – if the mouse is disconnected or missing, or faulty.

- A message on the screen – telling you of the problem.

Resolving problems

Sometimes when things go wrong, you will be able to sort it out yourself. You can check your system and connect any cables that are disconnected, change the fuse in a plug, switch the computer on if necessary or put paper in the printer tray.

Other times you may need help. If you are at work you need to know who to contact when you have a problem. It may be someone in your office, or you may have an IT Helpdesk that you can phone or email. You might need to fill in a form, or give specific details about your computer, e.g. its type or its serial number. Before reporting a problem, try to make sure that you can give as much information as necessary. Make a note of the problem, including any messages or error indicators from the system, and be able to explain what you were doing when the problem occurred. All these things will help in diagnosing the problem.

If you are at home, you might need to contact your supplier or your local computer shop for help. Again, you will need to be able to explain the problem to them as fully as possible.

It is worth making a note of the type of computer you have, the operating system you are using, the applications that you are running, the type of printer that you have, etc. so that you have this information to hand should you need to call someone. This information will be on the invoices that you have for your computer, or it can be found in the System Information panel (we will discuss this in Chapter 2).

1.17   A changing world

The world of computers never stands still. From the time that I have written this book, until the time that you read it, there will be new developments and innovations.

To find out more, and keep up to date, you can:

+ Read articles on developments in ICT in the newspapers.
+ Buy and read computer magazines.
+ Watch technology programmes on the TV.
+ Surf the Net.

Summary

This chapter has introduced you to the world of ICT – a rapidly changing and exciting environment. We have discussed:

+ The history of computers

+ Hardware

+ Software – operating system and application packages

+ Information networks

+ Health and safety issues

+ Hardware and data security

+ Legal considerations

+ System maintenance

+ Keeping up to date.

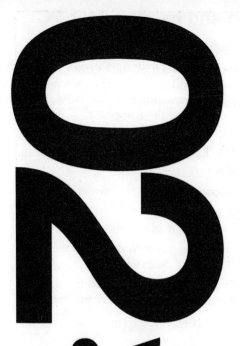

02

windows essentials

In this chapter you will learn

- how to start, stop and restart your computer
- about the Desktop
- how to manage your files
- how to use the online help

2.1 Start, stop and re-start your PC

Switching on the computer

The exact location of the switches on a PC varies from model to model. Have a look at your PC and try to find the switches. The switch on the main unit (the box containing the hard drive, CPU, modem, etc.) will be somewhere on the front of it.

The switch for the VDU (if it has one) will most probably be on the front of the unit, but it may be up the side or even on the back.

1 Ensure that your PC is plugged in and the power is switched on at the socket.

2 Press the ON/OFF button on the main unit.

3 Switch on the screen (if necessary – with some PCs the screen is switched on and off with the main unit).

Your computer may have been configured to display the **Welcome Screen** when it boots up, or the **Classic Logon** screen.

The Welcome Screen below has been set up for 4 users.

♦ Simply click on your user name.

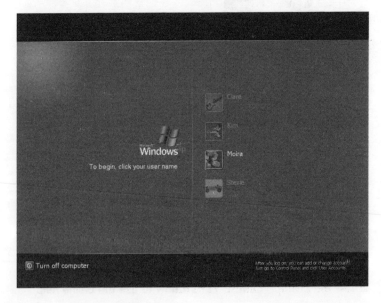

With a classic logon screen:

1 Enter your user name.

2 Enter your password.

3 Click **OK**.

Your computer will display the *Desktop* (see section 2.2) ready for you to tell it what you want to do next.

If you switch on your computer and it doesn't work, do some basic checks before calling for help. Check that:

- The cables are inserted into the back of the units properly.
- The computer is plugged in.
- It is switched on at the wall.
- The brightness control hasn't been turned down (there should be a control somewhere on your screen).
- The screen saver hasn't just blanked the screen (move the mouse and wait a few seconds to see if your PC wakes up!).

Log off or turn off the computer

- If you want to leave the computer on, ready for someone else to use, you should *log off*.
- If you have finished working on your computer altogether, you should *turn it off*.

To log off:

1 Close all your files and programs.

2 Click **Start** on the Taskbar.

3 Click **Log off**.

4 At the prompt, choose **Log off**.

- Windows will save your settings and return to the logon screen.

If there are several users set up on your PC, the Switch User option allows them to use the PC without you logging off.

To turn off your computer:

1 Click the **Start** button on the Taskbar.

2 Choose **Turn off computer**.

3 At the prompt, choose **Turn off**.

Standby puts the computer into hibernation mode, where it uses less power. Programs and files can be left open while in standby – so everything is up and running for when you want to start using the PC again. But beware, if there is a computer malfunction or a power failure, the data in memory may be lost – so I would recommend that you save and close your files before leaving the PC in standby mode.

There may be times when your computer 'hangs' and refuses to do anything. You may be able to restart it when this happens.

To restart the computer:

1 Click **Start**.

2 Choose **Log off**.

3 Select **Restart**.

If this is not an option, press the Restart button (usually located on the front of your CPU).

If all attempts to restart the computer fail, you will just have to switch it off (either at the on/off switch on the CPU, or at the wall if that fails) and try again!

2.2 The Desktop

The *Desktop* is the name given to the background of the screen.

Desktop icons can be moved. 'Drag and drop' them (click and hold down the left button, drag the icon to its new position and release the button), or get Windows to arrange the icons on the Desktop and position them automatically:

1 Right-click (click the right mouse button) anywhere on the Desktop.

2 A pop-up menu appears. Click (the left button) on the menu item **Arrange Icons By**.

3 Click **Name**, **Size**, **Type** or **Modified** as required.

Or

♦ Click **Auto Arrange**.

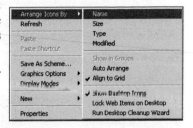

Icons – shortcuts to applications, folders or files

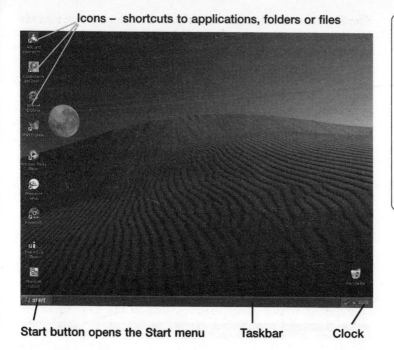

Start button opens the Start menu   Taskbar   Clock

The Start menu

The Start menu is used to launch applications, get Help, etc.

To open the Start menu, click start.

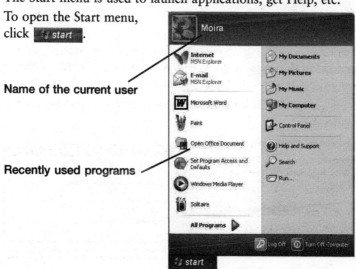

Name of the current user

Recently used programs

The Start menu gives a list of useful places on your PC, e.g. My Documents, Control Panel and Help and Support. It also gives easy access to the Internet and email, and your most frequently used programs (this is automatically updated as you use the PC).

The All Programs option will display a list of all the applications on your computer (not just the frequently used ones).

2.3 Working with windows

When you look at My Documents or at the Control Panel, the information is displayed in a window. When you open an application it will be displayed in a window.

It is important that you can recognize, name and know the purpose of the different parts of a window.

You should also know how to move and manipulate windows.

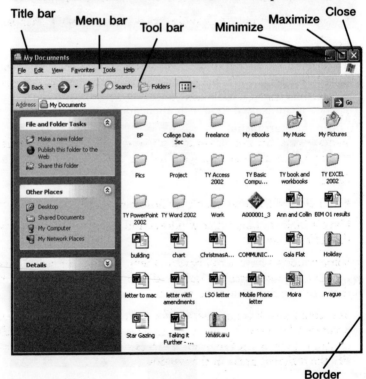

Title bar
Menu bar
Tool bar
Minimize
Maximize
Close

Border

Open *My Documents* so that you have a window to explore.

1 Open the **Start** menu (click **Start**).

2 Click **My Documents**.

Maximize/restore down

If a window is maximized it fills the whole screen – you cannot see any Desktop area behind it.

* To maximize a window click the **Maximize** ▣ button. It will be replaced by the **Restore Down** ▣ button – click this to reduce the window to its size before it was maximized.

Minimize/restore

When you minimize a window, it is tucked away so that can see whatever is behind it – perhaps the Desktop, or another application window. All that is then visible is its name on the Taskbar.

* Click the **Minimize** ▬ button to minimize a window.

* To restore a minimized window click its name on the Taskbar.

Resize

If a window is not maximized you will be able to see its border. Drag its border to make the window larger or smaller. The mouse pointer becomes a double-headed arrow when over a border.

Move

Windows that are not maximized can be moved around the Desktop. Drag the title bar of a window to move it.

Close

* To close a window, click the **Close** button ☒.

Have a look at some other windows and see if you can identify the different areas.

Some windows have scroll bars on them. You use the scroll bars to move up and down (or right and left) to display information that can't be fitted onto the screen.

You could also have a look at WordPad (open the **Start** menu, point to **All Programs,** then to **Accessories** and click on **WordPad**) or Paint (**Start > All Programs > Accessories > Paint**) and identify the different areas in the window.

Moving between open windows

If several windows are open you can move from one to another.

Either

• Click on the name of the window on the Taskbar.

Or

• Hold down [**Alt**] and press [**Tab**] repeatedly. You will cycle through the open windows. When the one you require is displayed on the screen, release the keys.

Desktop shortcuts

If you use an application, folder or file regularly, you could create a *shortcut* to it from the Desktop so that you can access it quickly.

To create a shortcut on your Desktop:

1 Ensure that your Desktop is visible behind the Start menu or the My Documents window.

2 Locate the program in the **Start** menu, or the folder or file in *My Documents*, right-click on it and drag it onto the Desktop.

3 Release the mouse button.

4 A context menu will be displayed.

• If you have dragged a folder or file from *My Computer* or *Windows Explorer* – click **Create Shortcuts here**.

Or

• If you have dragged an application from the Start menu – click **Copy here**.

When you want to access the application, folder or file, all you need to do is double-click the shortcut icon on the Desktop.

To remove a shortcut from your Desktop:

1 Select it (click on it).

2 Press [**Delete**].

This deletes the shortcut but not the application, folder or file.

2.4 Menu bar

At the top of each window is the Menu bar. You can use this to access every command in that application. You can display the menus and select options using either the mouse or the keyboard.

Using the mouse

1 Click on the menu name to display the options in that menu.

2 Click on the menu item you wish to use.

Using the keyboard

1 Hold down [Alt].

2 Press the underlined letter in the menu name, e.g. [Alt]-[F] for the File menu, [Alt]-[V] for the View menu.

To select an item from the menu list either:

• Keep [Alt] held down and press the underlined letter in an option name to select it, e.g. O in the File menu to Open.

Or

• Use the up and down arrow keys on your keyboard until the item you want is selected, then press [Enter].

• Once a menu list is displayed, you can press the right or left arrow keys to move from one menu to another.

To close a menu without selecting an item from the list:

• Click the menu name again.

Or

• Press [Esc].

In addition to the menus, many of the features can be accessed using the toolbars or keyboard shortcuts.

2.5 The Control Panel

The Control Panel on your PC allows you to check and change the current system information and settings. Some of these are hardware and software related (and you shouldn't change these unless you know what you are doing). Others options allow you to customize your working environment – setting the time and date accurately, controlling the volume of your speakers, customizing your Taskbar, screensavers and Desktop. You should explore and experiment with these settings.

System information

Your computer will most likely consist of:

* A unit that contains the Central Processing Unit (CPU), RAM memory, modem, a hard disk (your C: drive), a CDRW or DVD drive (or a combined drive) and a 3 ½" diskette drive
* Keyboard
* Mouse
* Visual display unit (VDU)
* Printer
* Speakers.

There may be times when you need to know something about these devices. This is particularly the case when you intend to upgrade your software or hardware, or when speaking to someone about your hardware or software not performing well.

Do you know anything about the specification of your computer? If someone asked you how much RAM your computer had or what processor it used would you be able to tell them? You can find this information, in the **System Properties** dialog box.

The *General* tab contains basic system information about your PC.

The *Hardware* tab is used when you want to add new devices to your PC. You can also use it to display a list of the devices that are currently installed, and to change their properties or troubleshoot any problems.

This PC has the Microsoft Windows XP Home Edition operating system, a Celeron 2.2 GHz processor and 256 Mb of RAM.

To access System Information:

1 Open the **Start** menu.

2 Click **Control Panel**.

3 Select **Performance and Maintenance** (Home Edition).

4 At the **Pick a Task** list, choose *See basic information about your computer.*

Or

◆ Double-click the System icon (Professional Edition).

The **System Properties** dialog box will appear.

Dialog boxes

A dialog box looks similar to a window, but has no Minimize, Maximize/Restore Down buttons – you can't change its size. Dialog boxes are used to collect information or option choices from the users. They normally have an OK button, a Cancel button and sometimes an Apply button. If you change the information in a dialog box, click:

◆ **OK** to close the box and make the changes take effect

◆ **Apply** to apply the changes without closing the box

◆ **Cancel** to close the dialog box without any changes taking effect.

Date and Time

At the far right of the Taskbar you will notice the clock. If you move your mouse pointer over it, the current date will appear.

To switch the clock display on or off:

1 Right-click on an empty area of the Taskbar.

2 Choose **Properties...**

3 On the **Taskbar** tab of the **Taskbar and Start menu Properties**, select/deselect the *Show the clock* checkbox to switch the display on or off.

4 Click **OK**.

The date and time displayed on your clock should be accurate. If they are not, you can correct them:

1 Double-click on the time icon at the right of the Taskbar to open the **Date and Time Properties** dialog box. Make sure that you are on the **Date & Time** tab.

To change the month:

2 Click the drop-down arrow beside the month field.

3 Select the month.

To change the year:

4 Click the arrows to the right of the year field.

To set the date:

5 Select the date on the calendar.

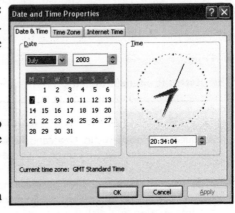

To set the time:

6 Double-click on the part of the time field that you wish to change – the hours, minutes or seconds.

7 Use the split arrows to the right of the field to increase or decrease the value as necessary, or type in the value required.

8 Click **Apply** or **OK**.

To change the time zone:

1 Click on the name at the top to open the **Time Zone** tab.

2 Choose the time zone required from the drop-down list.

3 Tick ☑ A_u_tomatically adjust clock for daylight saving changes to have your clock changed automatically each spring/autumn.

4 Click **OK**.

Volume settings

The volume settings used by your audio equipment may be controlled physically (by adjusting the volume on your hardware) or it may be possible to control the volume using software.

You can adjust the volume of the audio warning sounds (e.g. the one you hear when you try to close a file without saving it) from the Control Panel.

1 Open the Start menu.

2 Click Control Panel.

3 Select **Sounds and Audio Devices**.

4 Adjust the Volume settings using the **Volume** tab.

Or

• Explore the **Sounds** tab and select a **Sound Scheme** or the individual sounds required for programme events.

To toggle the display of the volume icon on the Taskbar:

1 Select **Sounds and Audio Devices**, then the **Volume** tab.

2 Select/deselect the **Place volume icon in the Taskbar** option.

3 Click **OK**.

4 Close the **Sounds, Speech, and Audio Devices** window.

If the volume icon is displayed on your Taskbar, you can change the volume of audio devices from there:

1 Click the Volume Control button on the Taskbar.

2 Increase or decrease the volume as required.

3 Click anywhere on your screen to close the volume control.

Appearance and Themes

You can change the way that your windows environment looks to suit your own preferences. The colour scheme, background, screen saver, user account picture, etc. can all be customized. When you log off, Windows will save your settings.

To access the Appearance and Themes options:

1 Open the **Start** menu.

2 Click **Control Panel**.

3 Double-click **Display**.

• The **Display Properties** dialog box will be displayed.

The Themes tab of the Display Properties dialog box. A theme sets the background image, the colours and fonts used in windows, menus and dialog boxes, and the warning sounds. All these can be set individually – a theme gives you a matching selection.

To customize the Desktop:

1 Select the **Desktop** tab in the **Display Properties** dialog box.

2 Scroll through the list and select a background.

3 Specify the display option – *Centre*, *Tile* or *Stretch*.

4 Click **Apply** (if you want to keep the dialog box open) or **OK**.

• If you select **None** in the background list, you can choose a colour for your Desktop from the colour options.

To set a screen saver:

1 Select the **Screen Saver** tab in the **Display Properties** dialog box.

2 Click the drop-down arrow and select a saver from the list.

3 Click **Settings**, adjust the screen saver options as required and click **OK**.

4 Increase or decrease the **Wait time** as required (between 2 and 10 minutes is fine).

5 If you want to check your settings click **Preview**.

6 Click **Apply** or **OK**.

To change your user account picture:

1 Double-click **User Accounts** in the Control Panel.

2 Pick the account that you want to change.

3 Click **Change My Picture**.

4 Scroll through the pictures and select the one required.

5 Click **Change Picture**.

2.6 Keyboard language

By default your keyboard language is most likely to be English. If you have others using your keyboard and their primary language is not English, you can adjust its settings according to the language required.

To add another keyboard language:

1 Click the **Start** button and choose **Control Panel**.

2 Open **Regional and Language Options**.

3 Select the **Languages** tab.

4 Click **Details** to display the **Text Services and Input Languages** dialog box.

5 On the **Settings** tab, click **Add...** to display the **Add Input Language** dialog box.

6 Scroll through the list and select the input language required.

7 Click **OK** to add the language.

8 Click **OK** at the **Text Services and Input Languages** dialog box to confirm your selection.

9 Click **OK** at the **Regional and Language Options** dialog box.

◆ The Language bar should be displayed in the Notification area of the Taskbar. To change your keyboard layout, click the Language bar and select the language from the list. If the Language bar is not displayed, you can switch it on from the **Text Services and Input Languages** dialog box – click **Preferences** and select **Show the Language Bar on the Desktop**.

2.7 Help and Support Center

The Help and Support Center is a central point from which you can get access a huge amount of information to support you as you work.

To access the Help and Support Center:

◆ Open the Start menu.

◆ Choose 🔘 Help and Support . The Home page of the Help and Support Center will be displayed.

You can interrogate the Help system in a variety of ways.

To browse the Help system:

◆ Click the topic that you are interested in on the Home page.

Have a look at Windows Basics – you'll find lots of useful information in here!

To search for Help:

1 Type the word(s) that you want Help on in the **Search** field.

2 Click the **Start Searching** button, or press [**Enter**].

To use the Index:

1 Click 📖 Index .

2 Type in the keyword(s) to find, e.g. 'new folder'.

3 Press [**Enter**].

Type a word you want Help on

Start searching

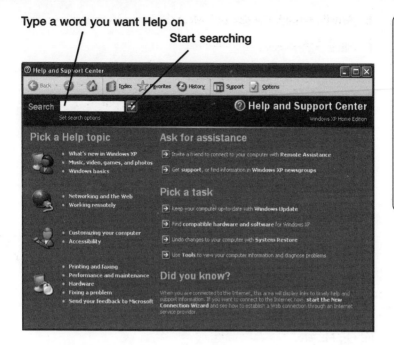

To return to a page that you've already visited:

◆ Click 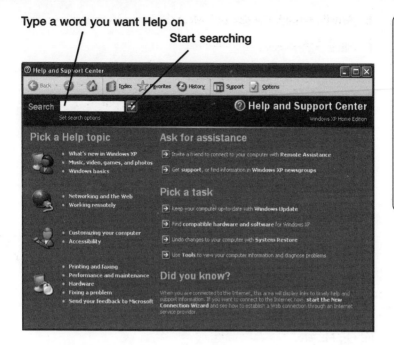 Back until you reach the page.

Or

1 Click History to display the list of pages already visited.

2 Select the page required.

3 Click Display.

◆ Once you've used Back to return to a page, you can use ➔ to go forward through the pages visited again.

Favorites

If you find a Help page that you know you will want to revisit regularly, you could add it to your Favorites

To add to Favorites:

1 Display the Help page required.

2 Click Add to Favorites.

To go to a Favorite page:

1 Click .

2 Select the page that you wish to go to.

3 Click **Display**.

◆ You can return to the Home page at any time by clicking on the toolbar.

Make the Help and Support Center one of the main areas that you visit – you'll learn a lot from it!

2.8 File management

The programs and data that are stored on your PC are stored on disks which are housed in drives. The drives are named using letters of the alphabet. Your diskettes use the A: drive. Your local hard drive is the C: drive. Your CD-ROM/DVD drive is probably your D: drive. You may have other drives, or there may be network drives available to you. They will be named E:, F:, G:, H:, etc.

We have already seen that you can display the contents of your computer system and disks in *My Computer*, and the contents of your own work area using *My Documents*.

As you increase the use that you make of your computer, you will eventually end up with lots of files in *My Documents*. It is important to organize them, so that you can find any file easily.

You can organize your files in much the same way as you would a manual filing system – by setting up folders for your work and storing your documents within the folders.

Online storage

In addition to local storage there are now several companies offering online storage facilities. The advantages of this are that the files can easily be accessed over the Internet so it is possible to share access to them with other users. It can also be used for off-site backups.

Folders and files

Imagine you are secretary of your local Wine Appreciation Society, and you've decided to create a new folder within My Documents for the files that you create for this important institution.

To make a new folder:

1 Display *My Documents*, or open the folder (double-click on it) that you wish to make a new folder within.

2 Click 🗀 Make a new folder .

3 Type in the folder name.

4 Press [Enter].

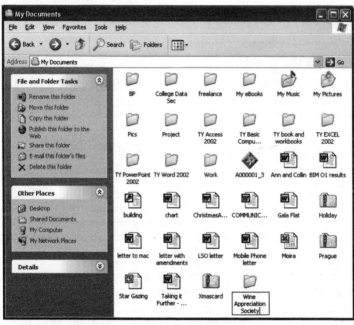

To display your folders/files using a different view:

1 Click the drop-down arrow by the **View** tool.

2 Select a view.

Details view gives information on the size, type and date that the file was modified, etc. You can sort the files into order on any column by clicking on the heading of the column.

File types

Different file types are created by different applications. You can identify a file's type from the icon by its name, e.g.

   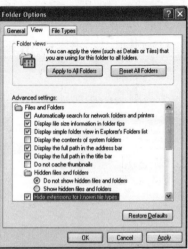

PowerPoint   **Word**   **Excel**   **Access**   **PDF**

or by the three-character extension at the end of the file name (if it is displayed).

You can toggle the display of the extensions:

1 Open the **Tools** menu in *My Documents* and choose **Folder Options...**

2 Select the **View** tab.

3 Scroll through until you find *Hide extensions for known file types*.

4 Select or deselect the checkbox as required.

5 Click **OK**.

You should be familiar with these common file extensions:

Extension	Application	File type
mdb	Access	Database
doc	Word	Word processing
xls	Excel	Spreadsheet
bmp	Paint	Image file
pub	Publisher	Desktop publishing
ppt	PowerPoint	Presentation graphics
htm/html	Various	Web page
pdf	Acrobat	Portable document format
wav, mp3, wma	Audio	Audio files
mpeg	Video	Video files
zip	WinZip	Compressed file
tmp	Various	Temporary files
exe	Various	Executable file
rtf	Various	Word processing

Working with files

To select an individual file/folder:

• Click on it.

To select several files/folders that are adjacent to each other:

1 Click on the first one.

2 Hold down [**Shift**] and click on the last in the set.

To select several non-adjacent files/folders:

1 Click on the first one.

2 Hold down [**Ctrl**].

3 Click on each of the other files/folders required.

You can rename a folder or file if its current name is unsuitable.

To rename a folder or file:

1 Select the folder or file.

2 Click [🖳 Rename this folder] (or **Rename this file**) in the **File and Folder Tasks** pane.

3 Type in the new name for the folder or file.

4 Press [**Enter**].

To move a folder or file:

1 Select the folder or file.

2 Click [🖳 Move this folder] (or **Move this file**).

3 Indicate where the folder or file is to be moved to.

4 Click **Move**.

To copy a folder or file:

1 Select the folder or file.

2 Click [🖳 Copy this folder] (or **Copy this file**).

3 Indicate where the folder or file is to be moved to.

4 Click **Copy**.

Backups

A very important way of trying to ensure the security of your data is to back it up. This means that you take a copy of any important data – anything that you can't afford to lose.

Companies often have automated backup procedures where their data is backed up every few hours, or overnight. If you are working at home, or in a small business, it will probably be up to you to remember to back up your data.

You should regularly copy any data files that are important to a removable storage device, e.g. a USB flash drive, an external hard drive or CD. On a home computer, the usual backup device is now a CD-RW. It is cheap, and stores 650 or 700 Mb of data.

Deleting a folder or file

This is a two-step process. When you delete a folder or file it is placed in the Recycle Bin. If you then realize that you should not have deleted it, you can restore it from there.

1 Select the folder or file.

2 Click ✗ Delete this folder (or **Delete this file**).

Or

◆ Press [**Delete**].

3 Confirm the deletion at the prompt – click **Yes** to delete, or **No** if you've changed your mind.

Recycle Bin

To open the Recycle Bin:

◆ Double click the Recycle Bin icon 🗑 on the Desktop.

To restore a folder/file from the Recycle Bin:

1 Select the folder or file(s).

2 Click 🗑 Restore this item in the **File and Folder Tasks** pane.

The item will be removed from the Recycle Bin and returned to the folder it was deleted from.

To restore all items that are in the Recycle Bin:

♦ Click **🥅 Restore all items** .

To empty the Recycle Bin:

♦ Click **🗑 Empty the Recycle Bin** .

Compression

Some files, particularly those that contain graphics and lots of formatting, can become quite large. If you have plenty of room on your disk this poses no problem, but if you are short of disk space you could *compress* the file to make it smaller.

If you want to send a large file to someone – either by email or by copying it onto a floppy disk – you might need to compress it to make it smaller.

You can compress a file from the **File Properties** dialog box.

1 Open the folder that contains the file you want to compress.

2 Right-click on the file and choose **Properties**.

♦ Note the *Size* and *Size on disk* fields – they will be fairly similar.

3 Click **Advanced** in the **Attributes** options.

4 Select the *Compress contents to save disk space* checkbox.

5 Click **OK** to return to the **Properties** dialog box.

6 Click **OK** to close the **Properties** dialog box.

♦ Display the **Properties** dialog box again, and note the difference between the *Size* and *Size on disk* fields. The *Size on disk* field will be smaller than the *Size* field.

♦ Repeat steps 1–6, deselecting the checkbox at step 4, to uncompress a file.

Searching for folders or files

If you have forgotten which folder you put your file into, you should be able to find it using the Search option.

1 Open the **Start** menu.

2 Click **🔍 Search** .

- The Search Results window is displayed.

3 Choose what you want to search for, e.g. **Documents**.

You can search on different criteria, or a mixture of criteria.

4 Enter all or part of the document name.

5 If you know a key word or phrase that occurs in the document, enter it into the appropriate field.

6 Tell the search which drive or folder you want to look in.

In addition you can...

7 Specify the date.

8 Give an indication of document size.

9 Click *Use advanced search options*, then:

- Choose whether or not to search subfolders, or

- Indicate whether or not the filename is case-sensitive.

10 Click **Search**.

A list of the files that match your criteria will be displayed. Once you've found the file, double-click on it to open it.

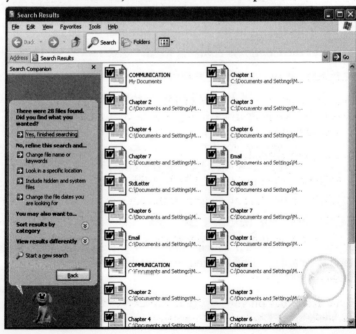

Searching for specific file types

If you want to display all the Word files or Excel files, you can do so easily as long as you know your file extensions (see page 62). Type the extension in the *All or part of the document name* field, e.g. '.doc'. When the search is complete, the files of that type will be displayed, together with the total number found.

Wildcards

When searching for files and folders, you can use *wildcards* to represent individual characters or strings of characters that may be variable from file to file.

'?' is used to represent an individual character.

'*' is used to represent a string of characters.

If you wanted to search for all the files on a drive or in a folder that had *report* in the filename – but you could not be sure where it might come in the name, you could use wildcards. In the filename field you could enter '*report*'. This would return all file that had *report* somewhere in the name, e.g. *End of term report*; *Report on marketing trends*; *Monthly report from Joe*.

A search string of 'Chapter ?' would return *Chapter 1, Chapter 2, Chapter 3*, etc.

Sorting

You can quickly sort the list of files in a folder in a variety of ways – ascending or descending order – by name, size, type or data modified.

To sort your file list:

1 Display the list using the **Details** view.

2 Click the heading at the top of the column that you want to sort on – the list will be sorted into ascending order.

3 Click the heading again to sort the list into descending order.

Read-only files

If you have files on your PC that you don't want changed, you can make them *read-only*. They can be opened but not edited.

To make a file read-only:

1 Display *My Documents*.

2 Right-click on the file you want to make read-only.

3 Choose **Properties**.

4 On the **General** tab select the **Read-only** checkbox.

To make a file read/write again, simply deselect the Read-only checkbox on the General tab.

2.9 Using a text editing application

The most common use of a computer is probably word processing, using Word or WordPad, or a similar application.

In this section we will take a *very* brief look at WordPad. WordPad is part of Windows and can be found in **Accessories**. It may be a pretty basic word processing package by today's standards, but it has all the features that you need to create, edit and print letters, reports and essays – and it is free!

To open WordPad:

1 Click the **Start** button and then **All Programs**.

2 Select **Accessories**.

3 Click **WordPad**.

A new file is created automatically, and all you need to do to produce your letter or report is start typing.

Text entry and edit

Your text will appear at the insertion point – the flashing black vertical bar in the document area.

• When entering your text, keep typing when you reach the end of the line on the screen – the text will wrap onto the next line automatically.

• Press **[Enter]** between paragraphs (press it twice to leave a blank line between the paragraphs).

• To delete a mistake, move the insertion point until it is next to the error (use the arrow keys on the keyboard or the mouse). If the insertion point is to the *left* of the error, press [Delete] to remove it. If the insertion point is to the *right* of the error, press **[Backspace]** to remove it.

• To insert something that you have missed out, move the insertion point until it is where the text is missing – and just type – existing text will be pushed along to make room for whatever you type in.

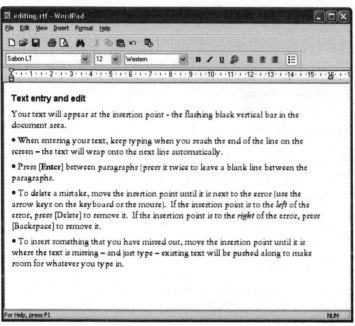

Microsoft Word is discussed in Chapter 4 – many of the basic formatting options discussed there are very similar in WordPad.

To save your file:

1 Click the **Save** tool ![save icon] on the Standard toolbar.

2 Specify the drive and/or folder that the file should be stored in – *My Documents* will be the default.

3 Give the file a name.

4 Click **Save**.

To preview your document:

- Click the **Preview tool** 🔍 on the toolbar.

To print your document:

- Click the **Print tool** 🖨 on the Standard toolbar – one copy of the file will be sent to your default printer.

To create a new document:

1 Click the **New tool** 🗋 on the Standard toolbar.

2 Select the **New Document** type, e.g. Rich Text Format

- If you have a document open already, WordPad will prompt you to save it if you haven't already done so. Otherwise it will close any open file when you create a new one. Only one document can be open at a time in WordPad.

3 Click **OK**.

To close WordPad:

- Click the **Close** button ❎ at the right of the title bar.

Recently used files

Once you have started using your applications properly, you can quickly open any file that you have been working on recently without even opening the application.

1 Open the **Start** menu.

2 Choose **My Recent Documents**.

3 Click the file that you want to open.

2.10 Printers

Windows has 'plug-and-play' technology which allows it to recognize many printers and install them automatically. It doesn't always work, so you should know how to install one yourself.

To install a printer:

1 Connect the printer to your computer following the manufacturer's instructions.

2 Open the **Control Panel**.

3 Choose **Printers and Other Hardware**.

4 Click **Add a Printer**.

5 Follow the instructions on the screen.

Default printer

Your computer system may be set up so that you can print your files to one of several different printers – a laser, an inkjet, etc. When you print a file from an application it uses the *default* printer – the one that's been set up for your normal printing. You can change the default printer. The printer that you want to become the default must be installed before you do this.

1 Open the **Control Panel**.

2 Choose **Printers and Other Hardware**.

3 Choose **Printers and Faxes**.

4 Right-click on the printer that you wish to set as the default.

5 Select **Set as Default Printer**.

The default printer will have a tick beside it.

To manage the print queue

If you have sent several files to print, you may want to check on the progress of your files. You can display a list of files that are in the print queue.

1 Open the **Control Panel**.

2 Open **Printers and Faxes**.

3 Double-click on a printer to display the print queue.

You can use the menus in the print queue window to pause printing, purge print jobs (empty the queue), etc.

* To pause or resume printing of an individual document, right-click on it and select the option from the menu.

* To pause or resume printing of all documents sent to a printer, right-click on the printer and select the option from the menu.

Print screen

If you want to take a printout of exactly what is on the screen of your computer:

1   Press [Print Screen] (usually to the right of the function keys on your keyboard).

Or

   Press [Alt]-[Print Screen] to capture the active window.

2   Go to a document (in WordPad or Word) or run Paint.

3   Open the **Edit** menu and click **Paste**.

4   The document can be printed in the normal way, or from Paint you can save the screenshot as an image.

2.11   Virus protection

A virus is a program that gets loaded onto your computer without you realizing it. Once on your computer, viruses can spread throughout your disks, memory and files and cause all sorts of damage – and many of them can spread across networks and bypass security systems (see Chapter 8 for more information on types of virus and how they are transmitted).

To help ensure that your system is free from viruses you should install anti-virus software and run it regularly. Anti-virus software is not bundled with Windows, so it is up to you to source it yourself. Norton or McAfee are popular choices.

Anti-virus softare would normally be set up to check your system regularly, e.g. daily, but there may be times when you want to virus-check an individual file, folder or drive.

•   You should explore your anti-virus software and find out how you can virus-check individual files/folders as required, as it varies depending on the product and/or the version of the product installed.

It is important that you keep your virus software up to date as new viruses are being developed and released all the time. Anti-virus software suppliers are constantly updating their software and you will usually be entitled to free updates for a period, e.g. a year, depending on the software agreement you have with your supplier. You should make sure that you download the updates as they become available so that your system is well protected.

2.12   Installing software

Even if Windows XP and standard application software, e.g. Works or Office, were preinstalled on your computer when your bought it, you will most likely want to install new software at some stage – perhaps a game or desktop publishing software.

Nearly all new software is supplied on a CD, and installing it is usually an easy procedure.

1 Insert the CD into your CD drive.

2 Follow the instructions on the screen.

If the CD does not start the setup process automatically, check the package for instructions.

You will most probably be instructed to either:

1 Open the **Start** menu and choose **Run…**

2 Type 'D:setup.exe' into the **Open…** field (where D: is your CD drive).

3 Follow the instructions on the screen.

Or

1 Open the **Start** menu and choose **Control Panel**.

2 Select **Add or Remove Programs**.

3 Click **Add New Programs**.

4 Choose **CD** or **Floppy**.

5 Follow the instructions on the screen.

Ensure that you purchase your software from a reputable supplier. Pirate software is illegal, and may be a source of viruses.

Summary

This chapter has introduced you to essential basic Windows skills. You have found out about:

* Starting, stopping and re-starting your computer
* The Desktop and working with windows
* Menus
* Knowing your PC – system information, date and time, volume settings, themes, screen savers, etc.
* Keyboard languages
* Using the Help system
* Creating and managing folders
* Copy, move and delete folders and files
* Backups
* File compression
* Using WordPad
* Printers – installing, setting the default printer and checking progress of print jobs
* Print Screen
* Virus protection
* Installing software.

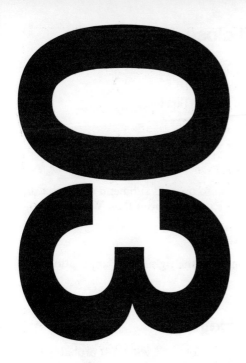

03

common skills

In this chapter you will learn

- about the online Help
- standard file handling and printing techniques
- how to format, search and spell check text
- about drawings and pictures
- how to manage toolbars

3.1   Open and close applications

1   Click the application icon on the Desktop, if present.

Or

2   Click the **Start** button on the Taskbar.

3   Choose **All Programs**.

4   Click the application if you can see it in the list, e.g. **Excel**.

Or

5   Point to a program group to open its submenu and select the application from there, e.g. **Accessories** then **WordPad**.

Closing an application

*   Click the **Close** button [x] at the right of the application title bar.

3.2   MS Office Help

As you work with your applications you will most probably find that you come a bit unstuck from time to time and need Help! There are several ways of getting Help – most of them very intuitive and user friendly. The Help system works in the same way in all Office applications.

If you have an Internet connection active, the Help system will integrate with the Microsoft website.

Office Assistant

To call on the Office Assistant:

1   Open the **Help** menu.

2   Choose **Show the Office Assistant**.

If you have a specific question you want to ask, type it in at the prompt and click the **Search** button.

The results will be displayed in the Search panel. Click on a result to display the Help page.

Click to show the text under this heading

Some Help pages contain text in a different colour.

* If the coloured text is embedded within the main text it is probably a phrase or some jargon that has an explanation or definition attached to it.

* Simply click the coloured text to display or hide the additional information.

When you've finished exploring the Help system, click the **Close** button at the top right of the Help window.

The Office Assistant can remain visible as you work on your file, or you can hide it and call on it as required. You can drag and drop it to reposition it on the screen.

* If you leave the Office Assistant displayed, click on it any time you want to ask a question.

- To hide the Office Assistant, right-click on it and choose **Hide** from the pop-up menu.

- To show it again, press **[F1]**, click, or open the **Help** menu and choose **Show the Office Assistant**.

- To change the way the Office Assistant works, right-click on it and choose **Options** from the pop-up menu. Set the options required in the **Office Assistant** dialog box.

Tips

The Assistant monitors your actions constantly. If it has a tip that may be useful to you, a bulb will light up beside it. To read its tip, click the bulb.

Type a question for help box

You can also access the Help system using the 'Type a question for help' box on the Menu bar. Type in your question and press **[Enter]**. Your results will be displayed in the Search Results pane – just click on the result that sounds most promising.

Help pane

Start searching

Whether or not you opt to use the Office Assistant, the Help tool or the Help menu option will open the Help pane. This is divided into three main sections.

Top – the search area, with an option to display the Table of Contents.

Middle – links to Office Online and areas that provide Help, training, etc.

Bottom – other useful links.

To search for Help:

1 Enter details of what you want in the **Search for:** field at the top of the pane.

2 Press **[Enter]** or click the **Start searching** button.

3 Select a result from the list displayed in the Search Results pane.

Alternatively, you can browse through the Help system.

1 Click **Table of Contents** at the top of the Help pane.

2 To open or close a book – click on it.

3 To open a Help page – click on it.

4 Browse the system until you find the Help you need.

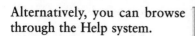

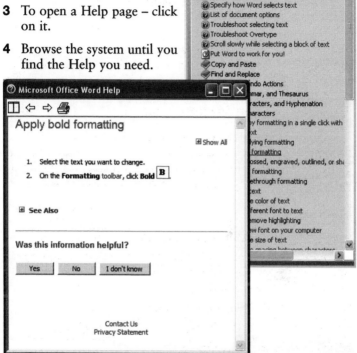

To tile the Help window with your document window:

◆ To be able to read the Help page while working on your file, click the **Auto Tile** tool [] to arrange the Help and document windows side by side on screen.

To revisit pages you've already been to:

◆ Click **Back** ⇦ or **Forward** ⇨ to move through the pages.

To print a topic:

◆ Click the **Print** tool in the Help window when the topic is displayed.

ScreenTips

If you point to any tool on a toolbar, a ScreenTip should appear to describe it. If no ScreenTips appear, you can switch them on.

1 Right-click on any toolbar and choose **Customize...**

2 In the **Customize** dialog box select the **Options** tab.

3 To switch the ScreenTips on, select the **Show ScreenTips on toolbars** option (or deselect this to switch them off).

4 Click **Close**.

Dialog box Help

When you access a dialog box, e.g. the **Customize** one, you can get Help on any item in it that you don't understand.

1 Click the Help button at the right of the title bar. The Help page for that dialog box will be displayed.

2 Follow the links to find the Help you need.

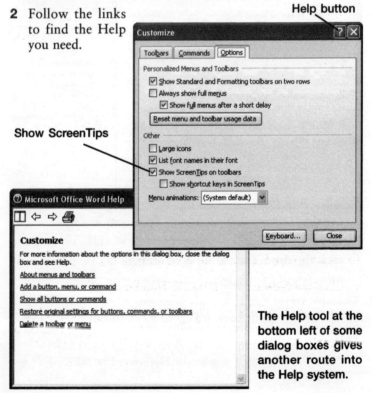

Help button

Show ScreenTips

The Help tool at the bottom left of some dialog boxes gives another route into the Help system.

3.3 File handling

File handling routines that are similar across applications include creating a file, opening, printing, saving and closing files.

The task pane

When you open an application, the Getting Started task pane for creating and opening files is usually displayed down the right of the window, and a new file is created. To work on the file, close the task pane (click its Close button) to give you more room for your file. You can open a file from the task pane – choose it from the list of file names or click the More... option.

If you don't want the Getting Started task pane to display when you start an application:

1 Open the **Tools** menu and choose **Options**.

2 Display the **View** tab.

3 Clear the **Startup Task Pane** checkbox in the **Show** options.

4 Click **OK**.

You can display the task pane at any time using the **View** menu:

1 Open the **View** menu.

2 Select **Task Pane**.

Create a new file

To create a new file using the default layout:

◆ Click the **New tool** ☐ on the Standard toolbar.

A new file will appear, e.g. *Document2*, *Book2*, (the number in the filename depends on the number of files you have created in this working session).

Open an existing file

To work on a file that you have closed, you must open it.

1 Click the **Open** tool [image] on the Standard toolbar.

♦ The **Open** dialog box will appear on your screen.

2 Locate the drive and/or folder in which your file is stored.

3 Select the file you wish to open – click on its name.

4 Click **Open**.

♦ You can open a file by double-clicking on its name in the **Open** dialog box.

If the file is a recently used one you will find its name displayed at the bottom of the **File** menu. You can open it from here, rather than go through the Open dialog box.

File	
Open...	Ctrl+O
Save As...	
Page Setup...	
Print...	Ctrl+P
1 C:\My Documents\...\Chapter 8.doc	
2 C:\My Documents\...\Chapter 5.doc	
3 C:\My Documents\...\Chapter 6.doc	
4 C:\My Documents\...\Chapter 4.doc	
¥	

1 Open the **File** menu.

2 Click on the filename.

If you wish to open more than one file simultaneously, select the files in the **Open** dialog box, and then click **Open**.

To select a group of adjacent files:

1 Click on the first file or folder.

2 Hold down [**Shift**] and click on the last file or folder.

To select several non-adjacent files:

1 Click on the first file or folder.

2 Hold down [**Ctrl**] and click on each of the other files.

Moving between open files

If you have more than one file and/or application open, you will see the names displayed on the Taskbar. If you point to the Taskbar button, the full file and application names will be displayed. To move to a file or application, click on its name.

♦ You can use the Window menu to go from one file to another within the same application – you will find a list of your open files at the end of it. Just click on the one you want.

Save and Save As

If you want to keep your file, you must save it. If you don't, it will be lost when you exit your application. You can save your file at any time – you don't have to wait until you've entered all your text or data and corrected all the errors.

1 Click the **Save** tool 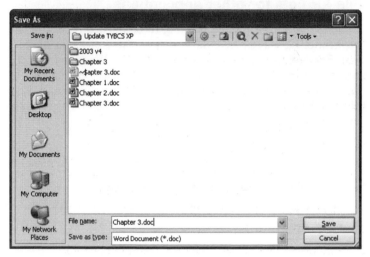 on the Standard toolbar.

2 At the **Save As** dialog box select the folder you want to save your file into.

3 Give your file a name.

4 Leave the **Save as type:** at the default, e.g. Word Document in Word, Microsoft Excel Workbook in Excel.

5 Click **Save**.

♦ The name of your file will appear on the title bar in place of the temporary filename.

As your document develops, you can re-save your file any time you wish – just click the Save tool again. The **Save As** dialog will not open, but the old version of the file on your disk will be replaced by the new, up-to-date version displayed on your screen.

There may be times when you save a file, edit it, then decide that you want to save the edited file but also keep the original version of the file on disk. If you don't want to overwrite the old file with the new version, you should save it using a different file name, or to a different drive and/or folder.

1 Open the **File** menu and choose **Save As**.

• The **Save As** dialog box will appear again.

2 Change the drive or folder if you wish.

3 Enter a new name in the **File name** field.

4 Click **Save**.

File formats for other applications

If the file you have created is going to be opened in a different application, it may be necessary to save it in a different file format. For example, if you have created a file in Word and you are going to send the text to someone who wants to open the file in Works, you should save the file in a Works format, or as a Text file, so that they can open it successfully. In some file formats some (or all) of the formatting may be lost.

To save in a different file format:

1 Click the **Save** tool or choose **Save As** from the **File** menu.

2 Select the drive and/or folder and name the file as usual.

3 Select the appropriate file format from the **Save as type** list.

4 Click **Save**.

3.4 Print and Print Preview

It is usually best to preview a file before you print it, so that you can check that it looks right before you waste paper and cartridges printing something that you later decide is unusable.

Print Preview

To preview a file:

• Click the **Print Preview** tool ⬛ on the Standard toolbar.

The preview screens of applications vary a bit, but you can usually move between the pages of a file, zoom in and out, change the Page Setup, e.g. margins, orientation, and print. We will look at areas specific to each application in the appropriate chapter.

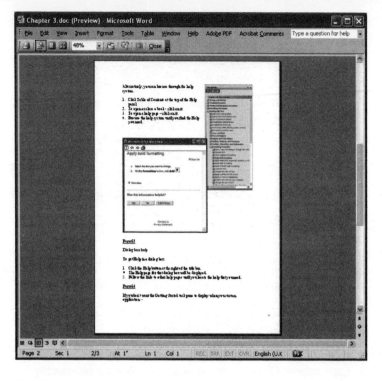

Print

To print one copy of your file on the default, click the Print tool ![icon] on the Standard toolbar. In some situations, particularly in an office environment, there may be several printers on the network that you can print to. Only one printer can be the default, but you can easily print to any other installed printer.

1 Open the **File** menu and choose **Print**.

2 Select the printer in the **Select Printer** area.

3 Set other options as required.

4 Click **OK**.

If you don't have a printer attached to your computer, or if you want to print your file out on a printer that doesn't have the application that you are using on it, you can print to a file. The file can then be printed out from any PC.

1 Open the **File** menu and choose **Print**.
2 In the **Select Printer** area select the printer to use.
3 Select the **Print to file** checkbox.
4 Click **OK**.
5 In the **Print to file** dialog box select the drive and or folder if necessary and give your file a name.
6 Click **OK**.

Closing files

Once you've finished working on a file you should close it.

◆ Open the **File** menu and choose **Close**.

Or

◆ Click the **Close** button at the top right of the file title bar.

You will be prompted to save the file if it has changed since the last time you saved it.

Smart tags

As you work with your applications you will notice that 'smart tags' appear at various times, e.g. when Word automatically changes something, such as capitalization, when you paste an item, when using automatic numbering, etc. If you click the smart tag it will display a list of options that allow you to control or customize the task that you are performing.

3.5   Delete, Cut, Copy and Paste

Delete

If you have a large piece of text or data to delete, it will usually be quicker to select it and then press [**Delete**] or [**Backspace**] rather than press them repeatedly.

To delete a chunk of text or data:

1 Select it.
2 Press [**Delete**].

Cut, Copy and Paste

There will be times when you have entered the correct information into a file but it is in the wrong place. When this happens you should move or copy the object, e.g. text in Word, data in cells in Excel, a picture or graph in any application, to the correct location.

◆ You can *move* an object from its current position, and place it somewhere else in the file (or another file).

◆ If you want to keep the object, but repeat it in another place in your file (or in another file), you can *copy* it.

You can move or copy an object within or between files. Before you can move or copy something you must select it.

To move or copy text:

1 Select the text that you want to move.

2 Click the **Cut** tool ✂ to move or the **Copy** tool ▤ to copy (they're on the Standard toolbar).

3 Position the insertion point where you want the object to go.

4 Click the **Paste** tool ▣ on the Standard toolbar.

The object will appear at the insertion point.

◆ To set the format of the pasted item, click the **Paste Options** smart tag (it appears below the item) and select the option.

Office clipboard

You can display the Office clipboard by choosing **Office Clipboard** from the **Edit** menu. The task pane displays a list of the items that you have cut or copied.

You can store up to 24 items in the Office clipboard.

To paste an individual item from the clipboard, click on it.

To paste all items, click **Paste All** at the top of the pane.

To empty the clipboard, click **Clear All** at the top of the pane.

To specify how you want the Office clipboard task pane to work, click the **Options** and set the options as required.

A Clipboard icon appears on the Taskbar when the task pane is displayed.

Click the **Close** button at the top right when you have done.

Cut or Copy to a different file

To move or copy an object from one file to another:

1 Open the file you want to move or copy the object from (the source).

2 Open the file to move or copy it to (the destination).

3 Display the source file.

4 Select the object you want to move or copy.

5 Click the **Cut** or **Copy** tool on the Standard toolbar.

6 Display the destination file.

7 Position the insertion point where you want the object to go.

8 Click the **Paste** tool on the Standard toolbar.

Drag and drop

As an alternative to using Cut or Copy and Paste to move and copy objects, try *drag and drop*. This is especially useful when moving or copying an object a short distance – i.e. to somewhere else on the screen. If you try to drag and drop over a longer distance, you will probably find that your file scrolls very quickly on the screen and that it is very difficult to control.

To move:

1 Select the object.

2 Position the mouse pointer anywhere over the object.

3 Click and hold down the left mouse button (notice the 'ghost' insertion point that appears within the selected area).

4 Drag the object and drop it into its new position.

To copy, hold down [Ctrl] while you drag the object.

Undo, Redo

To Undo an action:

• Click the **Undo** tool on the Standard toolbar.

Or

• Press [Ctrl]-[Z].

If you undo something by mistake, and want to redo it:

• Click the **Redo** tool ⌐ ▾ on the Standard toolbar.

3.6 Margins and orientation

Margins are the white space between the edge of the paper and the text/data area at the top, bottom, left and right of each page.

Orientation describes the way up that a sheet of paper is. The orientation can be portrait (tall) or landscape (wide).

You can easily change the margins and/or orientation of the pages in your file using the **Page Setup** dialog box.

1 Open the **File** menu and choose **Page Setup...**

◆ Word – Select the **Margins** tab, set the margins and/or orientation as required.

◆ Excel and Access – Select the **Margins** tab for the margins and the **Page** tab for the orientation.

◆ PowerPoint – use the **Page Setup** dialog box to specify the paper size and orientation.

2 Click **OK**.

3.7 Spelling and grammar

To help you produce accurate work, you can use the proofing tools to check the spelling and grammar in a file.

Check that you are using the correct dictionary for your proofing. In the UK, you would normally want to use the English (UK) dictionary rather than the English (US) dictionary.

To check or set the default dictionary (in Word and PowerPoint):

◆ Open the **Tools** menu, choose **Language**, then **Set Language...** to display the **Language** dialog box. The default dictionary will be highlighted. The default language is also displayed on the Status bar.

To change the default language:

1 Select the language required in the **Language** dialog box.

2 Click **Default...**

3 Click **OK** at the prompt.

◆ In Excel, open the **Tools** menu and choose **Options**. The language options are on the **Spelling** tab.

Check spelling and grammar as you type

You can let the application check your spelling and grammar as you work (Word and PowerPoint), or run a spellcheck at a time that suits you (all applications). *Check as you type* is operational by default – if it isn't on your system, someone has switched it off. To turn it on again, open the **Tools** menu, select **Options** and select the option on the **Spelling & Grammar** tab.

To deal with spelling errors:

Words that aren't recognized will have a red, wavy underline. To find out what Word or PowerPoint suggests as an alternative, right-click on the highlighted word.

- If you wish to change the word to one of those listed, click on the word that you want to use in the shortcut menu.

- If you choose **Ignore All,** the word will not be highlighted again in the document in this working session.

- If you choose **Add,** the word will be added to the dictionary, and recognized as a correctly spelt word from now on.

To deal with grammatical errors:

Any words, phrases or sentences that have unusual capitalization or aren't grammatically correct will have a grey wavy underline. When you right-click on the error, the application will display the problem, and suggest a remedy if it can. You can choose whether to change your text to that suggested or ignore the suggestion.

Check spelling and grammar when you are ready

You can easily check your spelling and grammar at any time using the **Spelling and Grammar** tool on the Standard toolbar.

- Click the **Spelling and Grammar** tool [ABC] to start the check.

The application will check the spelling and grammar in your file. Respond to the prompts as you see fit. When the checking is complete, a prompt will appear to tell you so.

- Click **OK** to return to your file.

3.8 Font formatting

One way of enhancing your text is to apply font formatting to it. Font formatting can be applied to individual characters in your file. The most commonly used options have tools on the Formatting toolbar – others can be found in the **Format > Font** (Word, PowerPoint and Access) or **Format > Cells** (Excel) dialog box. The Formatting toolbar varies a little from application to application – this one is from Word. The formatting options discussed here are available in all Office applications.

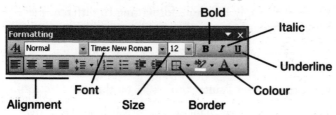

To format text or data as you type it in:

1 Switch on the formatting option(s) required.

2 Type in text or data.

3 Switch off or change the formatting option.

To apply or change the formatting of existing text or data:

1 Select the text or data.

2 Switch the formatting option required on or off, or apply an additional format, e.g

◆ To switch bold on or off, click the **Bold** tool 〔**B**〕.

◆ To switch italic on or off, click the **Italic** tool 〔_I_〕.

◆ To switch underline on or off, click the **Underline** tool 〔**U**〕.

Font styles, size and colour

The font style, size and colour are also easily changed.

To change the style of font:

1 Click the drop-down arrow by the Font tool 〔Times New Roman ▾〕 on the Formatting toolbar.

2 Scroll through the list of fonts and click on the font you want.

To change the size of font:

1 Click the drop-down arrow by the **Font Size** tool `12 ▾` .

2 Scroll through the list of sizes and click on a suitable one.

To change the colour of text:

1 Click the drop-down arrow by the **Font Color** tool.

2 Select the colour you want from the Font Color palette.

Format Painter

If you need to apply the same formatting to different pieces of text or cells throughout your file, you can use the Format Painter.

1 Select some text or data that has been formatted using the options you want to apply to other text.

2 Click the **Format Painter** tool ✧ on the Standard toolbar.

3 The mouse pointer changes to a brush icon. Drag over the text you want to 'paint' the formatting on to.

◆ If you want to paint the formats onto several separate pieces of text, double-click on the Format Painter to lock it. When you have finished, click the tool again to unlock it.

3.9 Paragraph/cell formatting

The default paragraph (Word/PowerPoint) or cell (Excel/Access) formatting options gives you a left-aligned text, with single line spacing. If this is not the formatting you want you can change it.

To apply formatting to a paragraph or cell as you type:

1 Set the formatting option required.

2 Enter your text.

To apply formatting to existing text:

1 Select the text or cell(s).

2 Apply the formatting required.

Alignment

To centre a paragraph, or text or data within a cell:

◆ Click the **Centre** tool ☰ on the Formatting toolbar.

To justify a paragraph (or paragraphs):

* Click the **Justify** tool ▤ on the Formatting toolbar.

To right align a paragraph (or paragraphs):

* Click the **Align Right** tool ▤ on the Formatting toolbar.

To left align a paragraph (or paragraphs):

* Click the **Align Left** tool ▤ on the Formatting toolbar.

Borders and shading

These formatting options can be very useful when it comes to emphasizing areas in your file.

To place a border around or between your paragraph(s) or cell(s):

1 Select the paragraph(s) or cell(s).

2 Click the drop-down arrow beside the **Borders** tool.

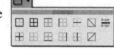

3 Select the border required.

To remove a border from your paragraph(s) or cells:

1 Select the paragraph(s) or cell(s).

2 Display the Borders options.

3 Click the **No Border** tool ▤.

There are more options in the **Borders and Shading** dialog box, including an outside border with a Box, Shadow or 3-D setting.

1 Display the **Format** menu and choose **Borders and Shading...** (Word) or choose **Cells** then go to the **Border** tab (Excel).

2 Experiment with the options.

3 Click **OK** or **Cancel** (to apply or abandon your changes).

To switch individual borders (left, right, top or bottom) on and off, click the border tools in the Preview window, or the lines around the edges of the example in the Preview window.

You can choose a shading effect for your paragraph(s) or cell(s). Select the **Shading** tab in the **Borders and Shading** dialog box in Word, or the **Patterns** tab in the **Format Cells** dialog box in Excel, and explore the options.

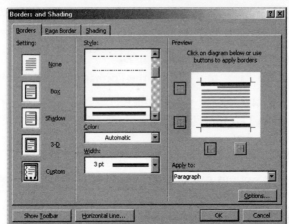

Preview - click on the border(s) then set the format

In Excel, border options are on the Border tab, and shading options on the Patterns tab of the Format Cells dialog box.

To format an individual border, click on its line in the Preview pane then pick a style and colour.

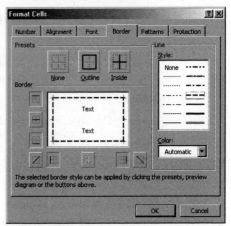

3.10 Find and Replace

The Find and Replace commands can be useful when working with longer files. **Find** allows you to locate specific text or data quickly. **Replace** enables you to find the specified text and replace it with other text – selectively of globally.

Find specified text:

1 Open the **Edit** menu and choose **Find...** (or press **[Ctrl]-[F]**) to display the **Find and Replace** dialog box.

2 On the **Find** tab, enter the text that you are looking for.

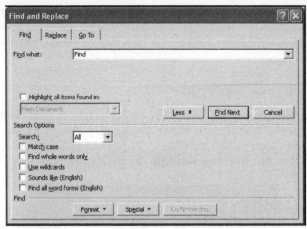

3 Click the **More...** button (Word) or the **Options...** button (Excel) if you wish to display the search options.

4 Select the options as required.

5 Click **Find Next**.

6 Continue clicking **Find Next** until you have located the text.

7 Click the **Cancel** button to close the dialog box.

Replace can be a very useful tool – especially if you've spelt a name wrong throughout a file!

1 Open the **Find and Replace** dialog box ([**Ctrl**]-[**F**]).

2 Select the **Replace** tab.

3 Enter the text you want to find in the **Find what:** field.

4 Specify any options and formatting as necessary.

5 Enter the text to replace it with in the **Replace with:** field.

6 Specify any options and formatting as necessary.

7 Click **Find Next**.

♦ The first occurrence of the text will be highlighted.

8 Click **Replace** to replace this one, then click **Find Next** again.

Or

♦ Click **Replace All** to replace all occurrences automatically.

♦ Experiment with the options and use the dialog box Help button as necessary to explore this feature fully.

Be careful when using Replace All – it may replace something that you didn't anticipate. Particular danger spots are numbers, which may be tucked away in a date, sum of money, address, etc.

3.11 Drawings

You can easily draw shapes and create images in your files using the Drawing toolbar. If it isn't displayed, you need to display it.

• Click the **Drawing** tool  on the Standard toolbar.

Drawing Canvas

A Drawing Canvas is placed around drawing objects when you create them. In Word, you can create the Drawing Canvas, then add objects to it, or insert the first object in your drawing and let Word automatically create the Drawing Canvas around it.

To create a Drawing Canvas:

1 Place the insertion point where you want your drawing.

2 Open the **Insert** menu.

3 Choose **Picture**.

4 Select **New Drawing**.

5 Create your drawing objects on the canvas.

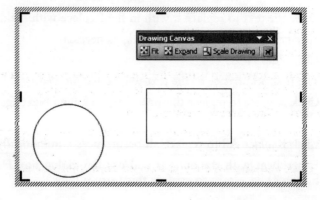

Or

1 Select one of the drawing tools.

2 Click, or click and drag to position the object.

♦ A Drawing Canvas is placed around the object and the Drawing Canvas toolbar is displayed.

Drawing Canvas toolbar options

Fit resizes the Drawing Canvas to fit neatly around the objects.

Expand makes the Drawing Canvas bigger.

Scale Drawing resizes/scales the Drawing Canvas and the objects within it (handles appear around the Drawing Canvas that you can drag to scale).

Text Wrapping specifies how the text in your document wraps around your drawing.

To align or distribute objects on your canvas:

1 Select the objects you you want to align or distribute from the Drawing Canvas.

2 Click the **Draw** tool on the Drawing toolbar.

3 Select **Align or Distribute**.

4 Choose an option.

	Group
	Ungroup
	Order ▸
	Align or Distribute ▸
	Rotate or Flip ▸
	Text Wrapping ▸
	Change AutoShape ▸

Align or Distribute submenu:
- Align Left
- Align Center
- Align Right
- Align Top
- Align Middle
- Align Bottom
- Distribute Horizontally
- Distribute Vertically
- Relative to Canvas

Draw ▾ | ⬚ | AutoShapes ▾

To format the Drawing Canvas:

1 Select the Drawing Canvas.

2 Open the **Format** menu.

3 Choose **Drawing Canvas**.

To create a drawing, position the insertion point where you want your drawing to appear and do one of the following:

To draw a line, arrow, rectangle or oval:

1 Click the line, arrow, rectangle or oval tool on the Drawing toolbar.

2 Click and drag where you want to draw your shape.

To draw a square or circle:

1 Select the **Rectangle** or **Oval** tool on the Drawing toolbar.

2 Click at the position you want the shape.

3 Hold down [Shift] and drag on a corner handle to make the shape larger or smaller.

To enter an AutoShape:

1 Click the **AutoShapes** tool AutoShapes ▾ on the Drawing toolbar.

2 Pick a category.

3 Select a shape.

4 Click on the Drawing Canvas to place your shape.

To add a text box:

1 Select the **Text Box** tool 🄰.

2 Click at the position you want the shape.

3 Type in your text.

4 Click outside the text box.

To add text to an existing box:

• Right-click on it and choose **Add Text**.

Editing drawn objects

If a drawing object is selected it has handles at each corner/along each side (squares). A selected object can be moved, resized or deleted. You can change the line styles or add a fill colour or special effect using the tools on the Drawing toolbar.

To move a shape:

• Place the mouse pointer within the shape and click and drag.

To resize a shape:

• Click on it then drag on a handle.

To delete a shape:

• Click on it then press [Delete].

To change a line style:

• Click the **Line Style** tool and choose a style.

To change line colour:

- Click the arrow by the **Line Color** tool ![line color icon] and pick one.

To change the fill colour:

- Click the arrow by the **Fill Color** tool ![fill color icon] and pick a colour.

To add a shadow:

- Click the **Shadow** tool ![shadow icon] and select an effect.

To add a 3-D effect:

- Click the **3-D effect** tool ![3d icon] and choose from the options.

When you draw shapes they are placed on layers – if you overlap them you will see the layering effect. You can change the order of the layers using the Order option in the Draw menu.

1 Select the shape(s) to move up or down the layers.

2 Open the **Draw** menu ![Draw menu icon].

3 Choose **Order**.

4 Select the **Bring Forward/Send Backward** option required to get the object to the required layer.

Rotate or Flip

- Use the **Rotate** or **Flip** options in the **Draw** menu to help you position your objects as required.

Group

Allows you to group a number of shapes into one, so that you can resize it and move it as if it were one shape.

1 Select the shapes – click on one, and then [**Ctrl**]-click on each of the others that you want to group together.

2 Open the **Draw** menu.

3 Choose **Group**.

Ungroup

Ungroups the selected shape.

Regroup

Regroups the ungrouped shapes (without having to select them again).

1 Select any one of the objects that was previously grouped.

2 Open the **Draw** menu and choose **Regroup**.

WordArt

WordArt gives you the option of creating special text effects.

1 Click the **Insert WordArt** tool 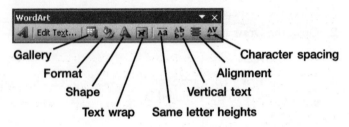 on the Drawing toolbar.

2 Select a WordArt style from the Gallery and click **OK**.

3 At the **Edit WordArt Text** dialog box, enter (and format) the text then click **OK**.

4 Adjust the shape of your WordArt object as required.

The WordArt toolbar

Gallery
Format
Shape
Text wrap
Same letter heights
Vertical text
Alignment
Character spacing

♦ Experiment with the tools to see the effects they produce.

3.12 Pictures

If you've installed Microsoft Office you'll find you've access to lots of clip art. If you've Internet access, you'll also find many more clips online.

To insert clip art:

1 Click the **Insert Clip Art** tool on the Drawing toolbar.

2 Leave the Search text box empty in the task pane to display all clips, or, enter a keyword to look for something specific.

3 Set the Search options, e.g. specify the collections and media file types (for clip art, search *All collections* in the **Search in** box, and choose *Clip Art* from the **Results should be** options).

4 Click **Go**.

5 Scroll through the list of clips displayed.

6 Click on the one that you want to use.

7 Close the task pane.

♦ The clip that you have chosen can be resized, moved or deleted using the same techniques as with drawings.

The clips that you insert into your document can be formatted in a number of ways – the best thing to do is experiment. When a clip is selected, the Picture toolbar is displayed. You can use the toolbar to modify your picture.

Working from left to right on the toolbar

Insert Picture inserts a picture from file rather than from the Microsoft Gallery.

Colour – *Automatic* is the default. *Greyscale* converts the colours to shades of grey. *Black and white* converts it to black and white only. *Watermark* converts it to a low contrast picture that you can place behind text to create a watermark.

More Contrast increases the contrast.

Less Contrast decreases the contrast.

More Brightness increases the brightness.

Less Brightness decreases the brightness.

Crop lets you trim the edges of the clip.

1 Click the **Crop** tool.

2 Drag a resizing handle to crop the bits you don't want.

Rotate Left – turns the picture through 90°.

Compress Picture – allows you to reduce the file size.

Line Style puts lines around the picture, or changes the line style.

Text Wrapping allows you to specify how you want your text to wrap around your picture.

Format Picture opens the **Format Picture** dialog box where you have access to even more formatting options.

Set Transparent Color – makes one colour transparent. This only works on bitmaps, GIFs and similar image formats. After clicking this, click on a part of the picture with the colour you want to make transparent.

Reset Picture returns the clip to its original state.

You can also edit the inserted clip art, e.g. change the colours.

1 Right-click on the picture.

2 Select **Edit Picture**.

3 The individual objects that make up the picture can now be selected.

4 Double-click on any object to open its **Format** dialog box.

5 Format the object as required and click **OK**.

6 Click outside the picture when finished.

If you have pictures on disk that are not in the Gallery (perhaps a photograph), you can insert them into a document.

To insert a picture from a file:

1 Open the **Insert** menu.

2 Select **Picture**.

3 Choose **From File...**

4 Locate the file to insert – explore the folders on your system.

5 Select the file and click **Insert**.

3.13 Zoom

Most files are displayed on your screen at 100% zoom – full size. You can zoom in on your file to get a closer look at something, or zoom out so that more of the file is displayed on the screen at any one time.

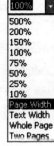

1 Click the drop-down arrow beside the **Zoom** tool.

2 Select the percentage zoom required.

3.14 Toolbars

Standard and Formatting toolbars: row sharing

If you don't want the Standard and Formatting toolbar to share one row, you can switch off the option that enables this feature. The Standard and Formatting toolbars can then be positioned on two rows – the Standard one above the Formatting one.

To toggle the row sharing option:

1 Click the drop-down arrow at the right of the Standard or Formatting toolbar.

2 Choose **Show Buttons in One Row** or **Show Buttons in Two Rows** as required.

Showing and hiding toolbars

Some toolbars appear and disappear automatically as you work. The Picture toolbar appears when a picture is selected, the WordArt toolbar appears when a WordArt object is selected.

You can opt to show or hide toolbars when you want to use the tools on them. If at least one toolbar is displayed, you can use the shortcut method to show or hide any toolbar.

To use the shortcut method:

1 Right-click on a toolbar.

♦ Any toolbars that are displayed have a tick beside their name.

2 Click on the toolbar name to show or hide.

If no toolbars are displayed, you must use the View menu to show them again.

1 Open the **View** menu and choose **Toolbars**.

2 Click on the one you want to show.

Using either of these methods, you can show or hide one toolbar at a time. If you want to change the display of several toolbars at once, it may be quicker to use the Customize dialog box.

1 Right-click on a toolbar.

Or

• Open the **View** menu and choose **Toolbars**.

2 Click **Customize...**

3 On the **Toolbars** tab, select or clear the toolbars as required (a tick means they are displayed).

4 Click **Close**.

Moving toolbars

Toolbars can be positioned anywhere on your screen. There are four docking areas – at the top, bottom, left and right of your screen, and your toolbars can be placed in any of them. You can also leave your toolbar floating in the document area.

The Standard and Formatting toolbars are normally displayed along the top of your screen, docked side by side, sharing a row.

To move a toolbar if it is docked:

1 Point to the line of dots at its left edge (if it is docked at the top or bottom) or top edge (if it is at the left or right).

2 Drag and drop the toolbar where you want it.

If the toolbar is not docked:

1 Point to its title bar.

2 Drag and drop the toolbar to the position you want it in.

3.15 Keyboard shortcuts

Some keyboard shortcuts are common to most applications, and it can therefore save you quite a bit of time in the long run if you learn and use them. Try the Ctrl alphabet!

Ctrl with	Effect
A	Select All
B	Bold
C	Copy
D	Depends upon the application: Font dialog box (Word); Fill Down (Excel); Duplicate (PowerPoint);
E	Centre align
F	Find
G	Go To
H	Replace
I	Italics
J	Justify
K	Insert Hyperlink
L	Left align
M	Left indent (Word)
N	New file
O	Open file
P	Print file
Q	Remove paragraph formatting (Word)
R	Replace
S	Save file
T	Hanging indent (Word)
U	Underline
V	Paste
W	Close active window
X	Cut
Y	Repeat the last action
Z	Undo

Summary

This chapter discussed features that can by used in any of the applications in Office. These features included:

* Opening and closing an application
* File handling – New, Open, Save, Save As, Preview & Print, Close
* Online Help
* Delete, Cut, Copy and Paste
* Margins and orientation
* Spell and Grammar checker
* Font formatting
* Paragraph/cell formatting
* Format painter
* Find and Replace
* Drawing toolbar
* Pictures – clip art
* Zoom
* Show, hide and move toolbars
* Keyboard shortcuts.

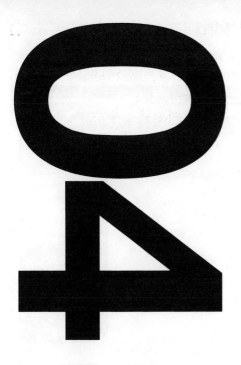

04

word processing

In this chapter you will learn

- basic Word skills
- about page layout
- how to use templates and styles
- about tables and graphs
- how to create a mail merge

4.1 Starting Word

When you start Word, a new blank document is displayed on the screen. Its name – *Document1* – is displayed on the title bar.

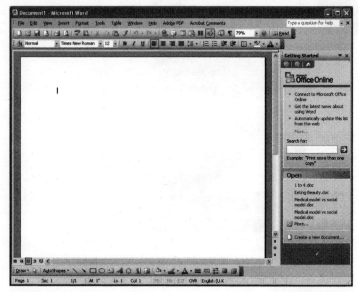

Each new document that you create during a session in Word is given a temporary name following the *Document1* format. Your second document will be called *Document2*, the next *Document3* and so on. These names should be considered temporary – you will save your document and give it a meaningful name instead of the temporary name assigned by Word.

If you want to start typing into a new blank document, simply click the Close button at the top right of the task pane to remove it from the screen and give you a larger document area. The insertion point – the flashing vertical bar – is in the top left of the text area on the first page. You're ready to start – just type!

Things to remember when entering text into your document:

- DO NOT press **[Enter]** at the end of each line. If a sentence is going to run onto a new line, let it – the text will be wrapped automatically at the end of the line.

- DO press **[Enter]** at the end of short lines, e.g. after lines in an address or at the end of a paragraph, or to create one or more extra blank lines between headings or in the signature.

4.2 Moving the insertion point

When you need to fix a mistake, the first thing you have to do is place the insertion point next to the error. If necessary, use the scroll bars to bring the text you want to edit into view.

There are several different ways of moving the insertion point.

Using the mouse

1 Position the I-beam (the name given to pointer when it is over a text area) at the place you want the insertion point.

2 Click the left mouse button.

Using the keyboard

◆ To move one character or line press [←], [→], [↑] or [↓].

◆ To move right or left a word press [Ctrl] and [←] or [→].

◆ To move up or down a paragraph press [Ctrl] and [↑] or [↓].

◆ To move to the end of the line press [End].

◆ To move to the beginning of the line press [Home].

◆ To move to the beginning of the document press [Ctrl]-[Home].

◆ To move to the end of the document press [Ctrl]-[End].

4.3 Editing

Insert and Overtype modes

Normally, when you type within existing text, the new text will push the existing text along to make room. This is Insert mode. In Overtype mode, new text will be typed over existing text, replacing it. You can easily switch between modes.

◆ When Overtype mode is on, the text on the Overtype button OVR on the Status bar is black.

1 Switch on Overtype mode – press [Insert].

2 Position the insertion point within some existing text and type – watch carefully to see what happens – the existing text will be replaced with the new text you enter.

3 Switch Overtype mode off again – press [Insert].

To insert new text:

1 Position the insertion point where you want the new text.

2 Type in your new text.

To delete existing text:

1 Position the insertion point next to the character that you want to delete.

2 To delete characters to the left, press [**Backspace**].

Or

♦ To delete characters to the *right,* press [**Delete**].

♦ Both [Backspace] and [Delete] repeat – if you hold them down they will zoom through your text removing it much quicker than you could type it in, so be careful with them!

To insert a new paragraph:

♦ Position the insertion point where the paragraph break should be and press [**Enter**] – twice if you want to leave a blank line.

To join two paragraphs:

♦ Press [**Delete**] after the first or [**Backspace**] at the start of the next to delete the break (produced by the [**Enter**] keypress) that separates them.

Page breaks

As you type in your text a page break is inserted automatically when you reach the end of your page. However, if you want a page break to occur at a specific point, e.g. at the end of a chapter or topic, you can easily insert a forced page break.

To insert a forced page break:

1 Position the insertion point where the page break is to go.

2 Press [Ctrl]-[Enter].

4.4 Selection techniques

Selection techniques are *very* important in Word. You need to use them if you want to:

♦ Copy or move text within a document.

♦ Copy or move text from one document to another.

- Change the formatting of existing text.
- Quickly delete large chunks of text.

There are several ways to select text in Word – try some out and use whatever seems easiest for you.

Using the mouse, to select:

- Any amount of text, click and drag over it, or click at start of text, hold down [Shift], click at end of text.
- A word, double-click on it.
- A sentence, hold down [Ctrl] and click anywhere within the sentence.
- A paragraph, double-click to the left of the paragraph *or* triple-click anywhere within it.
- The whole document, triple-click in the left margin.

To deselect any unit of text:

- Click anywhere within the text or on the background.

Using the keyboard, to select:

- A character or line at a time, hold [Shift] press [←], [→], [↑] or [↓].
- A word at a time, right or left, hold down [Shift] and [Ctrl] and press [←] or [→].
- A paragraph at a time, up or down, hold down [Shift] and [Ctrl] and press [↑] or [↓].
- To the end of the line press [Shift]-[End].
- To the beginning of the line press [Shift]-[Home].
- To the beginning of the document press [Shift]-[Ctrl]-[Home].
- To the end of the document press [Shift]-[Ctrl]-[End].
- The whole document press [Ctrl]-[A].

To deselect any unit of text:

- Press one of the arrow keys.

Don't be afraid to experiment with the different selection techniques. Many of the keyboard ones are much more efficient than the usual click and drag method.

4.5 Word options

When Word is initially set up on your computer, the default file location for documents is normally the *My Documents* folder.

Other options, e.g. unit of measure (for margins/ruler), whether or not to show the task pane on startup, and user information e.g. name/initials are also set.

You can easily change any of these from the **Options** dialog box.

To change the options currently set:

1 Open the **Tools** menu.

2 Click **Options...**

3 Explore the tabs to see the current options.

4 Edit any as required.

5 Click **OK**.

Changing the default folder (for Save/Open operations):

1 Open the **Options...** dialog box.

2 Display the **File Locations** tab.

3 Highlight **File Type, Documents...** and click **Modify**.

4 Select the folder that you want to become the default folder for save/open operations.

5 Click **OK**.

To change the units of measurement:

1 Open the **Options...** dialog box.

2 Display the **General** tab.

3 Select the **Measurement Units** required.

4 Click **OK**.

To update user information:

1 Open the **Options...** dialog box.

2 Display the **User Information** tab.

3 Update the name/initials as required.

4 Click **OK**.

4.6 Special characters and symbols

Most of the characters you want to type into your document are available through the keyboard. However, there may be times when you want a character that is not on the keyboard. You may find it in the **Symbols** dialog box. Here are some examples:

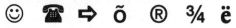

To insert a symbol:

1 Position the insertion point where you want the character.

2 Open the **Insert** menu.

3 Choose **Symbol**.

4 Select the font to use (spend some time exploring your fonts – Wingdings and Webdings contain picture characters).

5 Select a character – click on it.

6 Click **Insert**.

7 Click **Close** to close the dialog box.

4.7 View options

When working in a document, there are several view options. These control how your document looks on the screen – not how it will print out. You will usually work in Normal or Print Layout view.

Normal view

Normal view is often used for entering, editing and formatting text. The page layout is simplified – margins, headers and footers, multiple columns, etc. – are not shown.

To change to Normal view:

◆ Open the **View** menu and choose **Normal**.

Or

◆ Click the **Normal** view tool at the bottom left of the screen.

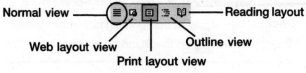

Print Layout view

In this view you can see where your objects will be positioned on the page. Your margins are displayed (and any headers or footers you have within them), and pictures, drawings, multiple columns, etc. are all displayed in their true position on the page. Print Layout view is useful if you are working with headers and footers, altering your margins, working in columns, or are combining text and graphics on a page and wish to see how they will be placed relative to each other.

To change to Page Layout view:

• Open the **View** menu and choose **Print Layout**.

Or

• Click the **Print Layout** tool at the bottom left of the screen.

Show/hide white space

The top and bottom margins are usually displayed as white space in Print Layout view. You can opt to show or hide this.

1 Go into Print Layout view (if necessary).

2 Move the mouse pointer to the top or bottom edge of a page.

3 Click when the **Show White Space** ⊞ or **Hide White Space** ⊞ prompt appears.

• The other view options are Web Layout, Outline and Reading Layout. You don't need to know how to use these views at this stage, but have a look at them if you wish.

Non-printing characters

Non-printing characters are those which affect the layout of your text, but don't print. For example, the characters inserted when you press the spacebar, [Enter], tab or non-breaking space character.

You can toggle the display of non-printing characters – you can opt to have them displayed on your screen or hidden. Either way they *do not* print – they are non-printing.

• To toggle the display of non-printing characters, use the Show/hide tool ¶ on the Standard toolbar.

4.8 Font formatting

Standard formatting routines are used when formatting characters in Word (see section 3.8). Explore the Font dialog box to see what other font formatting options are available.

1 Open the **Format** menu and choose **Font**.

2 Select the **Font** tab.

3 Choose the effects you want – a preview of your selection is displayed in the Preview window.

4 Click **OK** to apply the effects to your text, or **Cancel** to return to your document without making any changes.

In particular, explore the **Effects** on the Font tab, e.g. superscript, subscript, shadow, outline, emboss, etc. and the underline options in the **Underline** field.

Case change

If you type the correct text, but in the wrong case, e.g. upper case instead of lower case, you can change the case without having to retype the text.

To change the case of existing text:

1 Select the text.

2 Open the **Format** menu.

3 Choose **Change Case**.

4 Select the case required.

5 Click **OK**.

♦ The keyboard shortcut **[Shift]-[F3]** takes the selected text through lower case, Title Case and UPPER CASE.

4.9 Paragraph formatting

Some formatting options are applied to complete paragraphs, regardless of whether it consists of a few words or several lines. A paragraph is created in Word each time you press **[Enter]**.

The Alignment and basic Borders and Shading options were covered in the Common Skills chapter (section 3.9).

Borders and Shading

You can add and remove borders using the Border tool on the Formatting toolbar, or the Tables and Borders toolbar.

- Click the **Tables and Borders** tool 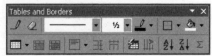 to toggle the display of the Tables and Borders toolbar.

To add borders to your text, paragraph or table:

1 Select the text, paragraph(s) or cells.

2 Choose a **Line Style** from the options.

3 Pick a **Line Weight** from those available.

4 Select a colour from the **Border Color** options.

5 Use the **Border** tool to specify where you want the border.

Line Spacing

Initially, the line spacing is set to single. You can set different spacing using the **Line Spacing** tool.

1 Select the text that you wish to change.

2 Click the drop-down arrow beside the **Line Spacing** tool.

3 Click on the line spacing option required.

To apply the most recently used line spacing option, simply click the Line Spacing tool (not the drop-down arrow).

Keyboard shortcuts

You can quickly set line spacing using keyboard shortcuts. Double line spacing [Ctrl]-[2], 1½ line spacing [Ctrl]-[5], single line spacing [Ctrl]-[1].

If you wish to set line spacing to a measurement other than one of those listed, click **More...** and specify your requirements in the **Line Spacing** field in the **Format Paragraph** dialog box (you can also access this dialog box from the **Format** menu).

Paragraph spacing

You can control the amount of spacing before and after a para-graph in the **Format Paragraphs** dialog box. This is useful if you want a specific amount of space above/below, or to leave a space between para-graphs without having to press [**Enter**] twice.

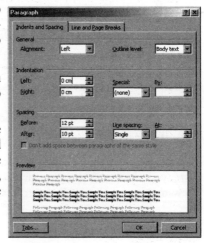

1 Open the **Format** menu and choose **Paragraph** to open the dialog box.

2 Set the spacing before and/or after the selected paragraph(s) – use the split arrows to adjust it, or type the value into the field.

3 Click **OK**.

Bulleted and Numbered Lists

You can add bullets or numbers automatically to paragraphs.

1 Click the **Bullets** tool to switch bullets on or off.

2 Click the **Numbering** tool on to switch the bullets or numbers on or off.

To change the bullet or number style:

1 Select the paragraphs.

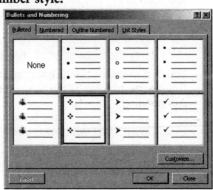

2 Open the **Format** menu and choose **Bul-lets and Numbering**.

3 Select the **Bulleted** or **Numbered** tab in the dialog box.

4 Choose a bullet or numbering option.

5 Click **OK**.

Indents

Paragraphs normally run the full width of the typing line – from the left to the right margin. As you enter your text, it extends along the line until it reaches the right margin and then it automatically wraps to the next line (unless you press [Enter]).

To increase the indent of a paragraph from the left margin:

• Click the **Increase Indent** tool ⊞ on the Formatting toolbar.

To decrease the indent of a paragraph from the left margin:

• Click the **Decrease Indent** tool ⊟ on the Formatting toolbar.

Indent markers

You can also use the ruler to set your indents. The ruler must be displayed along the top of your text area – if it's not, open the **View** menu and choose **Ruler** to display it.

The indent markers are the two triangles and the small rectangle at the edge of the ruler, and the small triangle at the right. Drag the appropriate marker along the ruler to set the indent.

To adjust the indent of:

• *The first line in the paragraph from the left margin*, drag the top triangle at the left edge of the ruler.

• *All other lines (except the first line) in the paragraph from the left margin*, drag the bottom triangle at the left edge.

• *All lines in the paragraph from the left margin*, drag the rectangle below the two triangles at the left.

• *All lines in the paragraph from the right margin*, drag the triangle at the right edge of the ruler.

To help improve accuracy when setting indents using the ruler, you can display the exact position of your indent on the ruler as you drag it along.

• Hold down [Alt] while you click and drag.

Alternatively:

1 Open the **Format** menu and choose **Paragraph...**

2 Select the **Indents and Spacing** tab.

3 Set the indents required in the **Indentation** fields.

4 Click **OK**.

Tabs

Tabs are used to align your text. If you want, say, a list of names and telephone numbers, you can use tabs to align each column.

The default tabs are set every 1.27 cm (half an inch) along the ruler – the small dark grey marks along the bottom edge of the ruler indicate their positions.

Each time you press [Tab], the insertion point jumps to the next tab position. The default tabs have left alignment – when you enter your text, its left edge will align with the tab position.

Tabs can be aligned to the left, right, centre or a decimal point.

Alignment	Effect	Possible use
Left	The left edge is at tab	Any text or numbers
Right	The right edge is at tab	Text, or numbers you want to line up on the unit
Centre	Centred under the tab	Anything
Decimal	Decimal point under tab	Figures to line up on the decimal point

If you need to use tabs and the pre-set ones are not what you require, you must set tabs at the positions you need them.

To set a tab using the ruler:

1 Select the type of tab – click the style button to the left of the ruler until you've got the required alignment.

2 Point to the lower half of the ruler and click – your tab is set.

↖ Tab style button

To move a tab:

* Drag it along the ruler to its correct position.

To delete a tab:

- Drag it *down* off the ruler, and drop it.

To set tabs in the Tabs dialog box:

1 Open the **Format** menu and choose **Tabs**.

2 Enter the **Tab stop position**.

3 Select the alignment.

4 Set a leader line or dots style if required.

5 Click **Set**.

6 Repeat until all your tabs are set, then click **OK**.

Hyphenation

Hyphenation can help to make line lengths similar throughout a document. It gives a document a more professional look by limiting the amount of white space left at the end of each line, and between words when the text is justified.

The easiest way to ensure that your text is hyphenated appropriately is to have the Automatic hyphenation option turned on.

1 Open the **Tools** menu, choose **Language**, then **Hyphenation**.

2 Select the **Automatically hyphenate document** checkbox, and set the other fields as required.

3 Click **OK**.

Manual line break

A manual line break ends the current line of text and continues your text on the next line. It *does not* start a new paragraph, but simply inserts a line break within the current paragraph.

- To insert a manual line break, hold [**Shift**] and press [**Enter**].

Manual line breaks are useful at the end of lines that use tabs to align columns of text or figures. If you separate the lines in your tabbed layout with manual line breaks, then move the tabs when the insertion point is within that layout, the whole column moves, not just the line with the insertion point (as would be the case if you created a new paragraph at the end of the line).

4.10 Print Preview and Print

See section 3.4 for standard preview and print information.

When you preview your file, a full page is displayed at a time. You can zoom in and out to read the text, and you can edit it.

Print Preview toolbar

The Print Preview window has its own toolbar which can be used to control the display of your document on the screen.

Experiment with the tools to see what effect they have. From left to right on the toolbar, you have:

Print

If you are happy with the appearance of your document, and want to print it, click the **Print** tool. One copy will be printed.

Magnifier

If you move your pointer over your page in Print Preview, you will notice it looks like a magnifying glass with a **+** on it.

* Position the pointer over your page and click the left button and you will be zoomed in and out of your document.

Editing text in print preview

If you zoom in on your text, and notice something that you want to change, you can edit your document in Print Preview.

* Click the **Magnifier** tool on the Print Preview toolbar. The insertion point will appear. Edit your document and click the **Magnifier** tool again so that you can zoom in and out.

One Page

Click this tool to display one page on the screen at a time.

Multiple Pages

This tool drops down a grid. Click and drag over it to indicate the number of pages you want to display at one time.

Zoom

Sets the percentage of magnification on your document.

View Ruler

Toggles the display of the vertical and horizontal rulers.

Shrink to Fit

If a small amount of text appears on the last page of your document you may be able to reduce the number of pages by clicking this tool. Word decreases the size of each font used in the document to get the text to fit on to one page less.

Full Screen

This removes most of the toolbars, menu bar, title bar, etc. to get a 'clean screen' display. To return to normal, click **Close Full Screen** on the **Full Screen** toolbar or press **[Esc]**.

Close Preview

Exits Print Preview and returns you to your document.

Moving through your document in Print Preview

If you have more than one page in your document, you can scroll through the pages in Print Preview to check them. To do this:

- Click the arrow up or arrow down at the top or bottom of the vertical scroll bar.

Or

- Click the **Previous** or **Next Page** buttons at the bottom of the vertical scroll bar.

Previous Page—

Next Page —

Print

If you don't want to print the whole document, you can specify the pages you want printed in the **Print** dialog box. You can also specify the number of copies you want printed from the dialog box.

1 Open the **File** menu and choose **Print**.

2 Select the **Page range** – *All*, *Current page* (the one the insertion point is in) or *Pages*, e.g. 1,2,4-7,12

- If you have selected some text before opening the dialog box, the **Selection** option is active so that you can print this text.

3 Set the number of copies required – usually 1.

4 Click **OK**.

4.11 Templates

A *template* is a pattern on which a document is based. You have probably been creating documents using the *Blank Document* template – you simply click the New tool on the Standard toolbar to create a document based on it. The document created has an A4 paper size, portrait orientation, 2.54 cm (1 inch) top and bottom margin, 3.17 cm (1.25 inch) left and right margin and single line spacing. Paragraph and character styles that are part of the Blank Document template are available in the style list on the Formatting toolbar (see section 4.12).

Word comes with other templates. You should look through them as you may find some useful. There are templates for letters, memos, fax, résumés (CVs) and many other types of document.

To create a document using a different Word template:

1 Open the **File** menu and choose **New** to display the **New Document** task pane.

2 Select **On My Computer** ... from the **Templates** list.

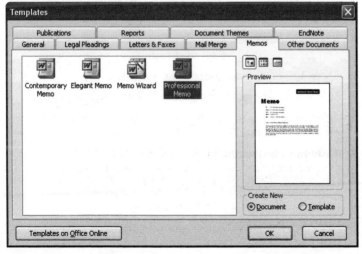

3 Explore the tabs in the **Templates** dialog box.

4 Choose a template.

5 Click **OK**.

Explore the document that you have created. Check out the layout – notice that some templates e.g. memo and fax, include areas for your company name, address, telephone number, etc.

Many of the documents created using a Word template include details on how to use and complete the new document. In the main, you just follow the instructions on the screen. Select and replace pieces of text that are used to prompt you for your own details e.g. 'Company name here'.

With other prompts, just do as you're told – click in the highlighted area and enter your information.

Your own templates

If you have a standard layout, e.g. your own memo or letterhead layout, you should save the basic layout as a template.

To create your own template:

1 Create a document based on a template and customize it as required, with your company name, address, etc.

Or

♦ Create a new blank document and set up the layout, standard text, etc. required for your template.

♦ Page Setup (section 4.13), headers and footers (4.14), styles (4.12), etc. can all be set up to suit your requirements.

2 Open the **File** menu and choose **Save As...**

3 In the **Save as type** field, choose Document Template.

4 Select the folder in which you wish to store your template – choose either the Templates folder or one of its subfolders.

5 Give your template a name and click **Save**.

Try out some of the templates on your system – they could help you produce a very professional looking document easily.

4.12 Styles

As an alternative to formatting text manually (using the Formatting toolbar or the dialog boxes) you could format it using a set of formatting options that have already been set up in a *style*. Each document will have several styles already set up. The text you have entered into your documents has been formatted using the *Normal* style – Times New Roman, size 12, left aligned.

To display the available styles:

♦ Click the drop-down arrow by the **Style** box on the Formatting toolbar to display styles in the current document.

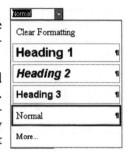

Many styles are already set up in Word – far more than those in the style list. Different styles are recorded in the various templates and are automatically available when you create a document using these.

To apply a style to new text:

1 Click the drop-down arrow by the Style box to open the list.

2 Select the style you want to use – click on it.

3 Type in your text.

4 Press [Enter].

Some sample styles

Heading 1 – Arial, size 14, bold, left aligned, spacing before 12 pt, spacing after 3 pt

Heading 2 – Arial, size 12, italic, left aligned, spacing before 12 pt, spacing after 3 pt

Heading 3 – Arial, size 12, left aligned, spacing before 12 pt, spacing after 3 pt

Normal – Times New Roman, size 12, spacing before and after 0 pt

When you press [Enter] after a Heading style, the style used for the *following paragraph* returns to **Normal** automatically.

To apply a style to existing text:

1 Select the text you want to apply a style to.

2 Click the drop-down arrow to the right of the Style box to display the style list.

3 Select the style you want to use.

> Styles are magic! They'll help you achieve a consistent look within and across your documents. You can also set up your own styles – check out the online Help.

4.13 Page Setup

You can change the Page Setup for all or part of your document. Initially, documents based on the default template consist of one *section*. If you select *Apply to: This Point Forward* when changing the page layout, Word creates a new section in your document. Each section can have different margins, orientation, page size, etc. If your document has more than one section the **Apply to:** field in the **Page Setup** dialog box has three options – *Whole document*, *This point forward* and *This section* – so that you can modify the layout of existing sections.

The number of the section that the insertion point is currently in is displayed at the left of the Status bar, Sec 1 beside the page number.

Margins

To change the margin setting:

1 Open the **File** menu and choose **Page Setup...**

2 Select the **Margins** tab.

3 Edit the margin fields as required.

4 Specify the area of your document you want to apply the changes to in the **Apply to:** field.

5 Click **OK**.

Orientation

The orientation of a page can be *Portrait* or *Landscape*. The default is portrait. You can change the orientation of your pages for all of your document or for part of it as required.

To change orientation:

1 Open the **File** menu and choose **Page Setup...**

2 Select the **Margins** tab.

3 Choose the orientation required.

4 Specify the area of your document you want to apply the changes to in the **Apply to:** field.

5 Click **OK**.

Page Size

If you are not printing onto A4 paper, you may need to change the page size setting so Word can format the pages correctly.

To change the page size:

1 Open the **File** menu and choose **Page Setup...**

2 Select the **Paper** tab.

3 Choose the **Paper Size** required.

4 Specify the area of your document you want to apply the changes to in the **Apply to:** field.

5 Click **OK**.

4.14   Headers/footers

Headers and footers are displayed at the top and bottom of each page and can contain things like page numbers, the author's name, the filename or the date that the document was produced.

To insert a header or footer:

1 Open the **View** menu.

2 Choose **Header and Footer**.

The insertion point moves to the header area and the **Header and Footer** toolbar appears. The main document text is dimmed.

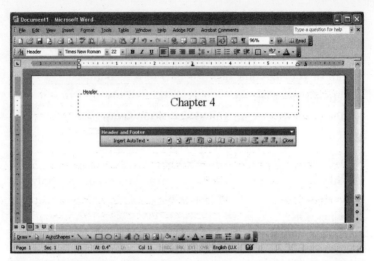

The header and footer area has a centre tab set in the middle of the line and a right tab at the end. You can use these to help you position your text and/or page numbers. You can type any text you wish into the header and footer areas. Use the tabs to help you position the insertion point as necessary.

You can format your text in the same way as you format text in the main document area.

Use the tools on the Header and Footer toolbar to insert fields that will be completed and updated automatically by Word.

Header and footer tools

Insert AutoText	Insert filename, author name, etc.
Insert page number	Inserts automatic page numbering
Insert number of pages	Inserts the total number of pages in the document
Format page number	Choose alternative formats for your page numbers
Insert date	Inserts the date that the document is printed

Insert time	Inserts the time that the document is printed
Page Setup	Displays the dialog box so you can set up header and footer options
Show/hide document text	Toggles the display of the document text
Same as previous	Makes/breaks link between headers and footers in different sections of a document
Switch between header and footer	Switches between the header and footer area
Show previous	Displays the previous header or footer in document (if document divided into sections)
Show next	Displays the next header or footer in document (if it is divided into sections)
Close	Returns you to your document

* You can also number pages by choosing **Page Numbers...** from the **Insert** menu and setting the options in the dialog box.

Always use headers and footers for text or numbers that you want on every page. *NEVER* type them into the main text area!

4.15 Tables

Tables are used to lay out text and data. Tables consist of rows and columns. Where a row and column intersect, we have a cell.

Row   Column

To create a table:

1 Place the insertion point where you want your table.

2 Click the **Insert Table** tool on the Standard toolbar.

3 Click and drag over the grid that appears until you get the number of rows and columns required.

4 Release the button – you have an empty table on your page.

You can move around a table using the keyboard or the mouse.

- Press [Tab] to move forward to the next cell.
- Press [Shift] – [Tab] to move back to the previous cell.

Or

- Click in the cell you want to move to.

Selecting cells in a table

- Click and drag over the cells you want to select.

Or

1 Click in the corner cell of the range you want to select.
2 Point to the cell in the diagonally opposite corner.
3 Hold down [Shift] and click.

To select a column:

- Click the top gridline or border of the column you want to select (you should get a black arrow pointing downwards).
- To select several adjacent columns, drag along the top border.

To select a row:

- Click to the **left** of the row you want to select .
- To select several adjacent rows, drag up or down the row selector area (to the left of the table).

To select a cell:

- Click just inside the **left** edge of the cell.

Click to select column

Click to select row

Other things to note

- When entering text into a cell, you will find that it automatically wraps once the text reaches the right edge, and the row deepens to accommodate the text you are entering (provided you've spaces between the words, or you pressed [Enter]).
- If you press [Tab] when the insertion point is in the last cell in the last row of your table, a new row is created.

- You can format your cells, or text within the cells, as normal, e.g. with bold, italic, colour, size, alignment (the text is aligned *within* the cell), borders and shading, etc.

Column width

In most cases, you won't want all your columns to be the same width – it depends what you're entering. You can easily change the column width. There are several methods you might like to try. The insertion point must be within a table when using these.

AutoFit

You must have some text or data in your columns to give AutoFit something to work on.

- Double-click the border or gridline to the right of the column whose width you want to change

Hotel	Address	Prices
Old Mill Inn	24 Mill Lane Melrose	Dinner £35, Single Room £30, Double Room £45
Kathy's Kitchen	12 High Street Duns	Lunch from £6, High Tea from £10/head

You will find a number of AutoFit options in the Table menu. Experiment with them to see how the different options work.

Manual adjustment

1 Position the pointer over the gridline or border to the right of the column.

2 Click and drag the border or gridline as required.

Or

- Click and drag the **Move Table Column** marker (on the ruler) which is above the right border of the column.

You can also adjust the column width from the **Table Properties** dialog box.

To display the dialog box:

1 Open the **Table** menu and choose **Properties**.

2 Select the **Column** tab.

3 Set the width and click **OK**.

Row height

You can adjust the row height in a similar way to column width.

To adjust manually:

1 Position the pointer over the gridline or border below the row you want to adjust.

2 Click and drag the border or gridline as required.

Or

• Click and drag the Row Marker on the vertical ruler.

You can also set the height in the **Table Properties** dialog box.

1 Open the **Table** menu and choose **Properties**.

2 Select the **Row** tab.

3 Set the height required and click **OK**.

Insert and delete rows and columns

To insert a row:

1 Select the row that will be below the new row.

2 Right-click on the selected area.

3 Choose **Insert Rows** from the shortcut menu.

To insert a column:

1 Select the column that will be to the right of the new column.

2 Right-click on the selected area.

3 Choose **Insert Columns** from the shortcut menu.

You may find that you have to adjust the width of your columns to accommodate the new columns you add.

To delete a row or column:

1 Select the row or column that you want to delete.

2 Right-click on the selected area.

3 Select **Delete Rows** or **Delete columns**.

To delete an entire table:

1 Place the insertion point anywhere inside the table.

2 Open the **Table** menu and choose **Delete**.

3 Click **Table**.

♦ If you select some cells in your table then press [**Delete**], the *contents* are deleted, but the table remains in place.

Table Autoformat

You can of course format the text, data and cells in a table using the Formatting toolbar and the dialog boxes.There are also some *Autoformats* that you can use to quickly format your table.

1 Click anywhere inside your table.

2 Choose **Table Autoformat** from the **Table** menu.

3 Select an **Autoformat** from the dialog box.

4 Select or deselect the checkboxes as required until you have the formatting options required.

5 Click **Apply**.

♦ Experiment with the tools on the Tables and Borders toolbar when working with your tables.

4.16 Mail merge

You can combine the text and/or layout of a standard document (e.g. letter) with a set of variables (usually names and addresses) to produce personalized documents using mail merge. The letters that you receive from banks, building societies and sales organizations, etc. promoting services and products, and personalized with your name and address, are often the result of a mail merge.

Mail merge jargon

The **main document** is the document that contains the layout, standard text and field names that point to the data source.

The **data source** is the file that contains the records you require for your mail merge – perhaps a name and address file. It is usually in a table layout – it could be a Word file or an Access or Excel table. We will create a data source in Word.

A **record** is the set of information on each item in a data source.

A **field** is a piece of data within a record. Title, surname, first name, telephone number, etc. would be held in separate fields.

A **field name** is the name used to identify a field.

The **result document** is the document produced when you combine the records in the data source with the main document.

There are three steps involved in mail merge:

1 Creating the **main document**.

2 Creating and/or locating the **data source**.

3 Merging the two to produce the **result document**.

If you are going to mail merge a letter, type and save it first. If you wish to use an existing file as the main document, open it. Use the Mail Merge wizard to step you through the process.

To set up the document and the data source:

1 Open the **Tools** menu.

2 Choose **Letters and Mailings,** then **Mail Merge.**

3 The **Mail Merge** task pane will be displayed.

4 At step 1, choose *Letters* as the document type, and click Next.

5 At step 2, choose *Use Current Document* – we are using the document that we have open, and then click **Next.**

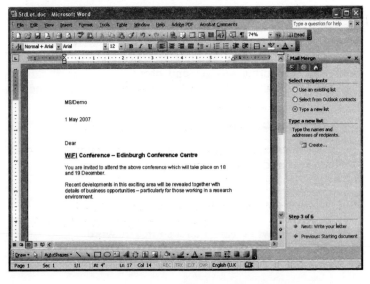

6 At step 3, choose *Type a new list*, then click **Create...** to set up the data source.

7 Add details of your address list into the data file.

8 Click **New Entry** when you have finished one record and want to enter another one.

9 Click **Close** when you have finished.

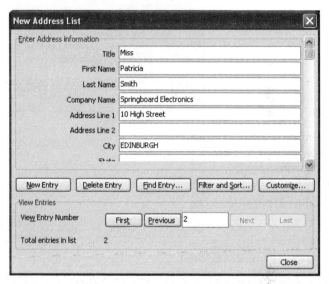

10 At the **Save Address List** dialog box, name the file and save it, then click **Next**. The List is saved as an Access database.

11 Click **OK** at the **Mail Merge Recipient** dialog box.

12 Click **Next** to go to step 4 of the Wizard.

To **set up the main document:**

1 At step 4, *Write your letter*, type in the letter (if needed).

2 Place the insertion point where you want the address and click **Address Block** in the task pane.

3 Select the options for your address and click **OK**.

4 Put the insertion point where you want the salutation and click **Greeting Line** – edit the set up as required and click **OK**.

5 If you have any more fields to insert, position the insertion point as necessary and click **More Fields...**

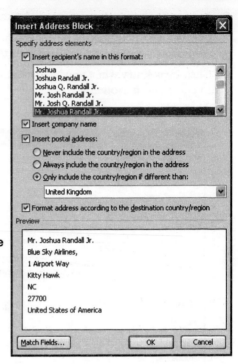

Use the Preview to see how your Address Block will look, as you set options

6 Insert the fields required.

7 Close the dialog box when finished.

To produce the Result document:

1 Click **Next: Preview your letters,** to see the results.

2 At step 5, use the buttons near the top of the task pane to move through your letters and check the layout.

3 If the layout is wrong, click **Previous** at the bottom of the task pane to return to step 4 and adjust the layout.

4 Click **Next: Complete the merge** to get to the final step.

5 If all letters are fine, click **Print...** to print them out.

6 If you wish to edit individual letters, click **Edit individual letters...** to create a result document that you can edit and print.

7 Close the task pane when you've finished.

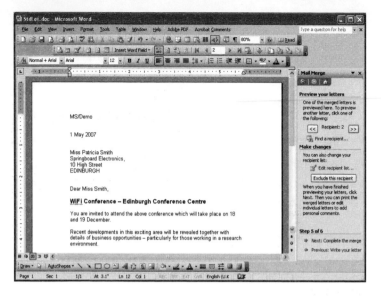

Mail Merge toolbar

If you are already familiar with mail merge, or you prefer not to use the wizard, you can use the Mail Merge toolbar. This appears automatically if you work through the Wizard. You can use the tools on this toolbar to work with your Mail Merge document.

From left to right:

◆ **Main document setup** sets a document as a main document.

◆ **Open Data Source** opens your name and address list – usually an Access database or Outlook Contact List.

◆ **Mail Merge Recipients** sorts and/or specifies recipients from the data source.

◆ **Insert Address Block/Greeting Line/Merge Field** all insert field names that link the main document to the data source information.

◆ **Insert Word Field** helps you control how Word merges in data. See 'About Mail Merge Field Codes' in the online Help.

◆ **View Merged Data** displays the results for the current record.

- **Highlight Merge Fields** shades the Merge fields.

- **Match Fields** allows you to select the field name in your data source that corresponds to the data that Word expects.

- **Propagate Labels** creates a sheet of labels from one definition.

- **First/Previous/Next/Last Record** all move through the records.

- **Find Entry** locates records where specified criteria are met.

- **Check for Errors** checks the field names and Word fields.

- **Merge to New Document/Printer/Email/Fax** are all destinations for the result document.

Editing the data source

Once opened, the data source can be edited. New entries may be added, obsolete ones removed, or existing records edited.

1 Open the data source file (if necessary).

2 Click **Mail Merge Recipients**.

3 Click **Edit...**

4 Edit, delete or add new records as required.

5 Click **Close**.

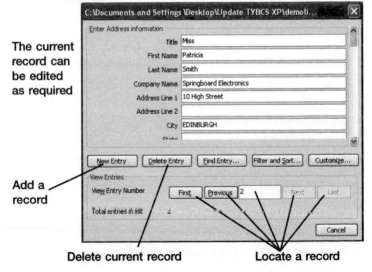

The current record can be edited as required

Add a record

Delete current record   Locate a record

Labels

This time, try creating labels using the Mail Merge toolbar.

1 Create a new blank document and display the Mail Merge toolbar (if necessary).

2 Click **Main Document Setup**.

3 Select **Labels**.

4 Choose a standard address label and click **OK**.

5 Click the **Open Data Source** tool and open your data file.

6 In the first label, click the **Insert Address Block** tool, or use **Insert Merge Fields** to build your label up field by field.

7 Once the first label is complete, click the **Propagate Label** tool .

8 Click **View Merged Data** to display your result document (or **Merge to a New Document** or **Printer** as required).

4.17 Charts

To create a chart in Word:

1 Open the **Insert** menu.

2 Select **Picture**, and then click **Chart**.

♦ The chart datasheet window will appear.

3 Enter the data that you want to create a chart from, into the datasheet (replace the sample data with your own).

4 When you've finished setting up your chart, click on your document, outside the chart area, to return to your document.

5 To edit an existing chart, double-click on it. The datasheet, Charting toolbar and Chart menu will appear again.

To insert or delete rows or columns:

1 Select the row or column (click the row number or column letter).

2 Right-click on the selected area.

3 Click **Insert** or **Delete** as necessary.

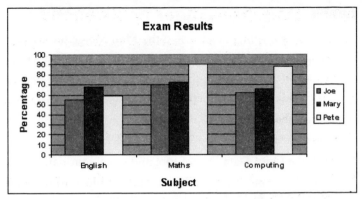

When you are working on your chart, you will notice that the Standard toolbar displays several tools for manipulating charts. Explore these tools and experiment with them to see their effects.

You will also notice that a **Chart** menu appears in the Menu bar – explore its options. There are two that you should try out!

- **Chart Type** – opens a dialog box that gives you access to a greater range of chart types and options than the **Chart Type** tool on the Charting toolbar.

- **Chart Options** – opens a dialog box that lets you add a chart title, add axis titles, move the legend, etc.

You can resize and move a chart just as you would any other object, e.g. a picture, in your document.

1 Click on the chart once to select it, then...

2 Drag a resize handle (in each corner and half way along each side) to make the chart bigger or smaller.

Or

3 Point to the middle of the chart and drag to move it.

To format an individual object within your chart:

1 Double-click on the chart to allow access to the datasheet, Chart toolbar and Chart menu.

2 Double-click on the object you want to format.

3 Select the options from the dialog box displayed.

4 Click **OK**.

4.18 Data from other applications

You can copy text, data, graphics, charts, etc. from one application to another in the Office suite using copy and paste.

1 Launch Word and the application you want to copy from.

2 In the other aplication, select the object, text or data you want to copy.

3 Click the **Copy** tool on the Standard toolbar.

4 Switch to Word.

5 Place the insertion point where you want the object, text or data to appear.

6 Click the **Paste** tool.

◆ If you copy and paste data from Excel, the data is displayed in a Word table.

4.19 Useful keyboard shortcuts

Keystrokes	Effect
[Shift]-[Ctrl]-[+]	Superscript
[Ctrl][=]	Subscript
[Ctrl]-[D]	Display Font dialog box
[Shift]-[F3]	Change case
[Shift]-[Ctrl]-[C]	Copy formatting
[Shift]-[Ctrl]-[V]	Paste formatting
[Ctrl]-[Shift]-[Spacebar]	Create a non-breaking space
[Ctrl]-[1]	Single line spacing
[Ctrl]-[5]	One and a half line spacing
[Ctrl]-[2]	Double line spacing
[F5] or [Ctrl]-[G]	Display the Find and Replace dialog box (Go To tab)
[Shift]-[Enter]	Manual line break
[Ctrl]-[Enter]	Manual page break

Summary

The chapter has introduced the features in Word that you should be able to use. We have discussed:

- The insertion point
- Editing
- Selection techniques
- Word options
- Special characters
- View options
- Font formatting
- Paragraph formatting
- Print and Print Preview
- Templates
- Styles
- Page Setup
- Headers and footers
- Page numbering – using headers and footers and using Insert, Page Numbers...
- Tables
- Mail merge
- Charts
- Importing data from other applications.

05

spreadsheets

In this chapter you will learn

- how to enter data in Excel
- how to adjust the size of rows and columns
- about writing formulae
- how to sort data
- how to create charts

5.1   Workbooks and worksheets

When working in Excel, the files that you work with are called *workbooks*. Each workbook consists of a number of *worksheets* (the default number is three). You can add more worksheets to a workbook if necessary, or remove any that you don't need.

Related data is usually best kept on separate worksheets in the same workbook – this makes it easier to find and manage them.

When you start Excel, you are presented with a new workbook displaying a blank worksheet. *If the workbook window is maximized, the workbook and the application share one title bar containing the application and workbook names.*

Worksheets

The worksheet tabs appear at the bottom left of your screen – to the left of the horizontal scrollbar.

To move from one sheet to another in your workbook:

♦   Click the sheet tab of the sheet you want to work on.

If you can't see all the sheet tabs in the bar, use the navigation buttons to the left of the tabs to scroll the other tabs into view.

To insert a new worksheet:

1   Select the worksheet (click on its tab) you want to have to the *right* of the new one.

2   Open the **Insert** menu and choose **Worksheet**.

♦   A new worksheet will appear to the left of the selected one.

If your workbook contains too many sheets, you can delete any that you don't need.

To delete a worksheet:

1   Select the sheet you want to delete.

2   Open the **Edit** menu and choose **Delete Sheet**.

Be careful when deleting sheets – Undo will not restore them!

By default, worksheets are named *Sheet1*, *Sheet2*, etc. You can rename the sheets with a name that actually means something.

To rename a worksheet:

1 Double-click on the sheet tab.

2 Type in the name you want to use.

3 Press [**Enter**] or click anywhere on the worksheet.

You can easily move or copy a worksheet within the workbook, or to another open workbook.

To move or copy a worksheet:

1 Select the worksheet you want to move or copy.

2 Open the **Edit** menu and choose **Move or Copy Sheet...**

3 Drop down the **To book:** list and choose the book to move or copy it to.

4 Select a sheet – this doesn't apply if you choose *new book* in the **To book:** field.

5 Tick **Create a copy** if you want to make a copy of the sheet, not move it.

6 Click **OK** – the sheet will be inserted before the selected one.

♦ If you move or copy your worksheet to a new book, remember to save the new workbook.

To move the worksheet within a workbook:

♦ Click and drag the worksheet tab of the sheet you want to move along the sheet tabs until it is in the correct place.

To copy the worksheet within a workbook:

♦ Click on the worksheet tab, hold [**Ctrl**] down and drag the worksheet tab to the required position.

5.2 Spreadsheet jargon

Before going any further, you need to learn some spreadsheet jargon. It's simple enough, once you know what it means!

The worksheet area consists of *rows*, *columns* and *cells*. Rows are identified by the numbers displayed down the left side of the worksheet area. Row 6 is highlighted in the illustration below. There are lots of rows on a worksheet – 65,536 in fact!

Address of active cell (Name box)

Formula bar

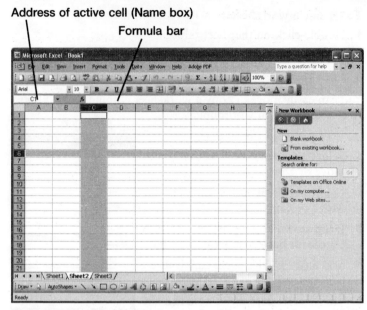

Columns are identified by letters displayed along the top of the
worksheet area. Column C is highlighted in the illustration. After Z, columns are labelled AA to AZ, then BA to BZ, and so on
to IV, giving 256 columns in all.

Where a row and column intersect you have a cell. Cells are
identified by addresses which consist of the column letter and
the row number. Cell A1, B9, C3, D6 and F3 are highlighted
here.

Text, data, formulas and functions

The cells in your worksheet will eventually contain text, numeric data, formulas or functions.

Text is used for titles or narrative to describe the figures you are presenting – worksheet headings, column headings and row labels will usually be text entries.

Numeric data means the figures that appear in your worksheet. The data may be entered through the keyboard, or it may be generated as the result of a calculation.

Formulas are used to perform calculations on the data in your worksheet. They are used to add the value in one cell to that in another or multiply the values in different cells, etc. Some formulas will be very basic while others may be quite complex.

Functions are predefined formulas that perform simple or complex calculations on your data. There are many different kinds of functions set up in Excel – statistical, logical, financial, database, engineering – and many more. You're bound to find some useful ones, whatever type of data you work with.

5.3 Moving around your worksheet

Before you can enter anything into a cell, you must make the cell you want to work on *active*. To make a single cell active, you must select it. You can easily move onto any cell (thus making it active) using either the keyboard or the mouse.

The active cell has a dark border. The address of the active cell appears in the Name Box to the left of the Formula bar.

To navigate with the mouse:

◆ Scroll the sheet to bring the cell into view if necessary and click into the cell to make it the active cell.

Navigation with the keyboard

To go to the next cell:

◆ Use the [←], [→], [↑] and [↓] arrows on the keyboard.

To move onto the cell directly below:

◆ Press [**Enter**].

To go to a specific cell address:

1 Press [F5].

2 Enter the address of the cell you want to go to in the **Reference** field of the **Go To** dialog box.

3 Click **OK**.

To go to cell A1:

• Press [Ctrl]-[Home].

To move to the end of your work area:

• Press [Ctrl]-[End].

Check out 'Keyboard shortcuts' in the online Help to see if there are any others that you would find useful.

5.4 Selection techniques

You will find that you often work on more than one cell at a time in Excel. You may need to format a group of cells in a particular way or copy or move a group of cells, or apply a function to a group of cells.

A group of cells is called a cell *range*. Cell ranges are identified by using the first cell address followed by a colon and then the last cell address in the group of cells you wish to work on, e.g. A1:A7, C3:D12, F5:H7 are highlighted in the picture below.

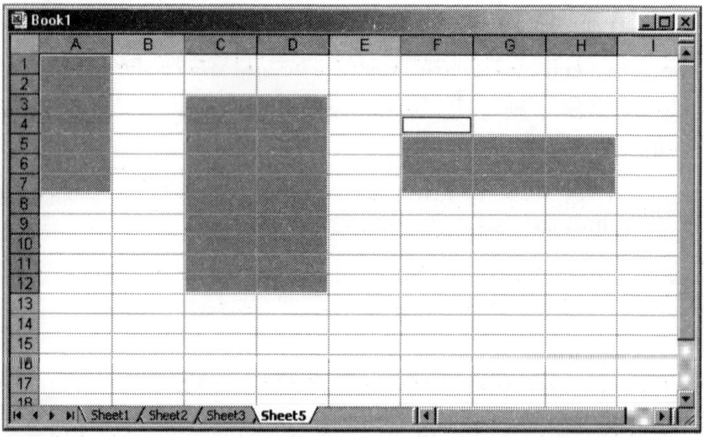

To select a group of adjacent cells:

♦ Click and drag.

Or

1 Click on a cell in one corner of the range.

2 Hold [**Shift**] and click on the cell in the diagonally opposite corner of the range.

To select a row:

♦ Click the row number to the left of the row you want to select.

To select several adjacent rows:

♦ Click and drag down over the numbers to the left of the rows.

To select a column:

♦ Click the column letter at the top of the column.

To select several adjacent columns:

♦ Click and drag across the letters at the top of the columns.

To select the whole worksheet:

♦ Click the box at the top left of the row and column headers.

To select a range of non-adjacent cells:

1 Click on one of the cells you want to select.

2 Hold [**Ctrl**] down and click on each of other cells.

To de-select a range of cells:

♦ Click on any cell in your worksheet or press an arrow key.

5.5 Entering text and numeric data

Entering text or data into your worksheet is easy.

1 Select the cell to enter text or data into.

2 Type in the text or data – it will appear in the Formula bar as well as in the active cell.

✗ ✓ ƒ Sales figures

3 Press [**Enter**] or click the 'tick' button to the left of the Formula bar when you've completed the cell.

Things to note when entering text

♦ Text automatically aligns to the left of a cell.

♦ Text that doesn't fit into a single cell will 'spill over' into the cell to the right if that one is empty.

• Excess text will not be displayed if the cell to the right is not empty. Widen the column (see section 5.6), reduce the font size or use a more compact number format to display it all.

Things to note when entering numeric data

• Numeric data automatically aligns to the right of a cell.

• If a cell displays ######## instead of the figures you will need to change the number format or adjust the column width to show all the data.

	A	B	C	D	E	F	G
1	Sales figures for 1st quarter						
2		January	February	March	Total		
3	Ann	£75,000.00	£52,000.00	£45,000.00	########		
4	Robert	£60,000.00	£65,000.00	£55,000.00	########		
5	Gill	£55,000.00	£70,000.00	£65,000.00	########		
6	Jackie	£86,000.00	£65,000.00	£75,000.00	########		
7	Jim	£90,000.00	£80,000.00	£80,000.00	########		
8							
9							
10							
11							
12							
13							
14							
15							
16							
17							

Sheet1 \ **Sheet3** / Sheet5 /

Editing text and numeric data

If you make an error when entering your work, you can fix things by deleting, replacing or editing the contents of the cell.

To delete the contents of a cell/s:

1 Select the cell (or cells) whose contents you want to erase.

2 Press [Delete].

To replace the contents of a cell:

1 Select the cell whose contents you want to replace.

2 Type in the text or data that should be in the cell.

To edit the contents of a cell:

1 Select the cell whose contents you want to edit.

2 Click in the Formula bar to place the insertion point in it.

Or

- Double-click in the cell, or press [**F2**] – this places the insertion point in it.

3 Edit the cell contents as required.

4 Press [**Enter**] when you've finished editing.

5.6 Adjusting columns and rows

All the columns are the same width unless you change them.

To change the width of a column manually:

- Drag the vertical line (in the heading row) to the right of the column, e.g. to change the width of column B drag the vertical line between columns B and C.

To adjust the column width automatically:

- Double-click the vertical line to the right of the column.

To change the height of a row manually:

- Click and drag the horizontal line below the number of the row whose height you want to adjust, e.g. to change the height of row 5 drag the horizontal line between rows 5 and 6.

To adjust the row height automatically:

- Double-click the line below the row.

You can also adjust the column width or row height from the Format menu.

If you need extra rows or columns in the middle of your working area, you can easily insert them. You can also delete rows or columns that you don't require.

To insert a row:

1 Select the row that will go *below* the row you are inserting.

2 Right-click within the selected area.

3 Choose **Insert** from the pop-up menu.

To insert a column:

1 Select the column that will go to the right of the column you are inserting.

2 Right-click within the selected area.

3 Choose **Insert** from the pop-up menu.

To delete a row or column:

1 Select the row or column you wish to delete.

2 Right-click within the selected area.

3 Choose **Delete**.

To add or delete several rows or columns at once:

1 Click and drag in the row or column label area to indicate the number of rows or columns you want to insert or delete.

2 Right-click within the selected area.

3 Choose **Insert** or **Delete** as required.

5.7 Fitting text into cells

When entering text into cells you might want to try some other formatting options to help you display your work effectively. These options can be used on any cells, but may be particularly

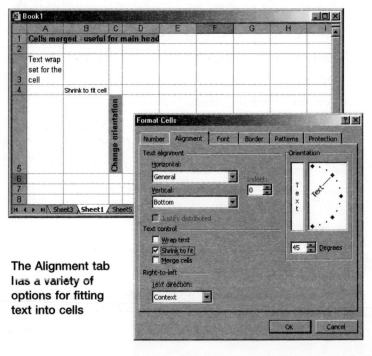

The Alignment tab has a variety of options for fitting text into cells

effective on column headings. Options include: merged cells, text wrap, shrink to fit, orientation and vertical alignment.

These options can all be found in the Format Cells dialog box, on the Alignment tab.

1 Select the cells you want to format.

2 Open the **Format** menu and choose **Cells...**

3 Select the **Alignment** tab.

4 Specify the option(s) required.

5 Click **OK**.

♦ You may need to adjust the row height or column width manually if it doesn't adjust automatically to accommodate the alignment options you choose.

5.8 Number formats

When entering currency values into a worksheet, you will usually want the appropriate symbol to precede the figure, e.g. a £ or Euro sign.

If you want the £ symbol in front of a figure you can either:

♦ Format the cells to display the entry in a currency format.

Or

♦ Enter the £ symbol through the keyboard.

If you enter your figures through the numeric keypad, it's probably easiest to format the cells to display the figures as currency.

You can format cells *before* or *after* you have entered your text or data.

To display the figures in currency format:

1 Select the cells you want to format.

2 Click the **Currency** tool 🔢 on the Formatting toolbar.

On UK keyboards, the keyboard shortcut for the Euro symbol is **[Alt Gr]+[4]**. If this doesn't work on your keyboard, check out "How to type the Euro sign" in the online Help.

The Formatting toolbar has other number formats – **Percent**, **Comma**, **Increase** and **Decrease Decimal**. Other formats can be found on the **Number** tab of the **Format Cells** dialog box.

To apply a format from the Format Cells dialog box:

1 Select the cells you want to format.

2 Open the **Format** menu and choose **Cells…**

3 Select the **Number** tab.

4 Choose a category from the list, e.g. *Currency*.

5 Complete the dialog box as required e.g. you may want to select a different symbol if the currency isn't £.

6 Click **OK**.

5.9 Freeze/unfreeze headings

Many of the worksheets you create will be considerably larger than will fit on to your screen. You will need to scroll vertically and horizontally to display the data you want to work with.

When you scroll through your worksheet, the column and row headings will disappear off your screen as other data appears. This is often very inconvenient, as you need to see the headings to make sense of your data. In a situation like this you should *freeze* part of your worksheet window so that it doesn't move, and scroll the unfrozen part of your window.

To freeze rows or columns:

1 Select the row below the ones you want to freeze.

Or

♦ Select the column to the right of the ones you want to freeze.

Or

♦ Select the cell below the rows and to the right of the columns that you want to freeze.

2 Open the **Window** menu.

3 Choose **Freeze Panes**.

When you scroll through your worksheet horizontally, the frozen columns remain in view. When you scroll through it vertically the frozen rows remain in view.

To unfreeze panes:

1 Open the **Window** menu.

2 Choose **Unfreeze Panes**.

5.10   Split screen

There will also be times when you want to compare the data on one part of your worksheet with that on another – but the data ranges are in separate areas of the sheet. When this happens, you should *split* your screen so that you can scroll each part independently, to bring the data you require into view.

If you look carefully at the top of the vertical scroll bar (above the up arrow), or to the right of the horizontal scroll bar (outside the right arrow), you will notice the *split box*. You must use the split boxes to split your screen.

To split your screen horizontally:

♦ Drag the split box at the top of the vertical scroll bar down to where you want your split to be.

To split your screen vertically:

♦ Drag the split box at the right of the horizontal scroll bar along to where you want your split to be.

When your screen is split, you can scroll each pane independently to view the data you want to see.

To remove a split:

♦ Double-click the split.

5.11   Formulas

Any cell which will contain a figure that has been calculated using other entries in the sheet should have a formula. Do *not* do your calculations on a calculator, then type in the answer.

Formulas allow you to add, subtract, multiply, divide and work out percentages of the values in cells.

Excel knows that a cell contains a formula if the first character it sees there is '='.

Operators used in formulas are:

   + Add   - Subtract   **/** Divide

   * Multiply   % Percentage

Formula examples

=A7/B6   Divide the figure in A7 by the figure in B6

=D22*12   Multiply the figure in D22 by 12

=C7*25%   Calculate 25% of the figure in C7

Order of precedence

If there is a mixture of operators, Excel will deal with multiplication and division *before* addition and subtraction, e.g.

=A4+C7*D7   Multiply the figure in C7 by the one in D7, and add the answer to the figure in A4

Parentheses (brackets)

Some formulas can become quite long and complicated. To force the order in which a formula is worked out, or make a long formula easier to read, you can use parentheses ( ). In this example, the problem within each set of parentheses is solved *before* working through the formula.

     =((A1+B2)*C3) - (D4/E5)

Add A1 to B2   we'll call this XX

Multiply XX by C3   we'll call this YY

Divide D4 by E5   we'll call this ZZ

Subtract ZZ from YY

Remember the BODMAS rule – Brackets over division, multiplication, addition then subtraction!

Entering formulas

You can enter a formula by typing it into the Formula bar, or by *pointing* with the mouse. Let's say that you wanted to enter the formula =B4-C4 into cell D4.

1 Select the cell, D4

2 Type '=' to tell Excel that the cell contains a formula.

3 Either type 'B4-C4'.

Or

- Click on B4 and its reference will be written into the formula, then type '-', and finally click on C4 to get its cell reference.

4 Press [**Enter**].

AutoFill

AutoFill can be used to copy formulas down columns or across rows. In the screenshot, the formula in cell D4 is =B4-C4. We need a similar formula in the other cells in the column.

To complete the cells using AutoFill:

1 Select D4.

2 Position the pointer over the bottom right corner of the cell. The Fill Handle – a small black cross – should appear.

	A	B	C	D	E	F	G	H
1	Furniture Sale - everything reduced by 60%							
2								
3	Item	RRP	Sale Price	Saving				
4	Desk	£ 300.00	£ 120.00	£ 180.00				
5	Cahir	£ 196.00	£ 78.40					
6	Table	£ 360.00	£ 144.00					
7	Bed	£ 400.00	£ 160.00					
8								
9								
10								

H ◄ ► H \ Sales Figures \ Cell formatting \ Sheet5 /

3 Click and drag the black cross over the other *Saving* cells.

When you release the mouse, the formula in cell D4 will be copied to the cells you dragged over.

If you click on each cell in the *Saving* column and keep an eye on the Formula bar, you will notice that Excel has automatically changed the cell addresses in the formula *relative* to the position you have copied the formula to.

You can also use AutoFill to automatically generate days of the week, months of the year or dates.

1 Enter 'January', 'Jan', 'Monday' or 'Mon' in any cell.

2 AutoFill it down or across.

To fill with dates:

1 Enter the first date in your series.

2 AutoFill using the *right* mouse button.

3 Select the Fill option (Days, Weekdays, Months or Years) required from the pop-up menu.

5.12 AutoSum

The worksheet below contains details of monthly sales figures.

	A	B	C	D	E	F	G	H
1		SALES FIGURES 1ST QUARTER						
2								
3	First name	Surname	January	February	March	Total		
4	Ann	Burns	£ 75,000	£ 52,000	£45,000	=SUM(C4:E4)		
5	Robert	Donaldson	£ 80,000	£ 65,000	£55,000	SUM(**number1**, [number2], …)		
6	Gill	McKenzie	£ 55,000	£ 70,000	£65,000			
7	Jackie	Munro	£ 86,000	£ 65,000	£75,000			
8	Jim	Andrews	£ 90,000	£ 80,000	£80,000			
9		TOTAL						
10								

Sales Figures / Cell formatting / Sheet5 /

To calculate the totals for each sales representative for the quarter and the total for each month, we could use a formula, e.g. =B4+C4+D4, but the easiest way to use *AutoSum*.

To calculate the totals using AutoSum:

1 Select a cell in which you want a total figure to appear, e.g. the cell that will hold the total sales for the first sales person.

2 Click the **AutoSum** tool $\Sigma \cdot$ on the Standard toolbar.

3 The range of cells to be added together will be highlighted. Note that the function also appears in the Formula bar.

4 If the suggested range of cells is correct, press [**Enter**].

Or

♦ If the suggested range is *not* the range of cells you want to add together, drag over the correct range, and press [**Enter**].

♦ Use AutoFill to copy the function down or across the other total cells.

If you are totalling rows and columns as in this example, you could use a shortcut to perform all the calculations in one move.

To AutoSum several groups of cells simultaneously:

1 Select all of the rows and columns you want to total, *and* the cells that will contain the results of the AutoSum calculations.

2 Click the **AutoSum** tool Σ ▾ on the Standard toolbar.

	A	B	C	D	E	F	G	H
	Book1							
1		SALES FIGURES 1ST QUARTER						
2								
3	First name	Surname	January	February	March	Total		
4	Ann	Burns	£ 75,000	£ 52,000	£45,000			
5	Robert	Donaldson	£ 80,000	£ 65,000	£55,000			
6	Gill	McKenzie	£ 55,000	£ 70,000	£65,000			
7	Jackie	Munro	£ 86,000	£ 65,000	£75,000			
8	Jim	Andrews	£ 90,000	£ 80,000	£80,000			
9		TOTAL						
10								

Sales Figures / Cell formatting / Sheet5 /

The cells in the rightmost column and bottom row of the selected area will each have the Sum function inserted into them.

You can also use AutoSum to total non-adjacent cells if you wish.

To total non-adjacent cells:

1 Select the cell that will contain the result of the calculation.

2 Click the **AutoSum** tool on the Standard toolbar.

3 Click on the first cell you want to include in the range.

4 Hold down [Ctrl] and click on each of the other cells to be included in the function.

5 Press [Enter].

If you prefer to type in the SUM function, start with '=' (equals).

A range of adjacent cells is defined by the address of the first cell, followed by a : then that of the last cell, e.g. **=SUM(B4:B10)**.

The addresses for non-adjacent cells must be separated by a ',' e.g. **=SUM(B4,C6,D9)**.

5.13 Statistical functions

Statistical functions include minimum, maximum, average, count – and many others. These can be used to display a value from a range of cells.

- To return the minimum value from a range use **MIN**.
- To return the maximum value from a range use **MAX**.
- To return the average value from a range use **AVERAGE**.
- To count the number of entries in a range use **COUNT**.

You can use the drop-down list beside the AutoSum tool Σ ▾ to display the functions.

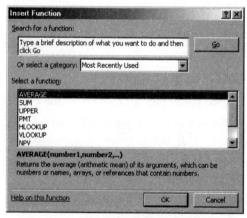

1 Select the cell that the function will go in.
2 Click the drop-down arrow at the right of the AutoSum tool.
3 Select the function. If it is not listed, click **More Functions**, explore the **Insert Function** dialog box and select it from there.
4 Check/amend the cell range as necessary.
5 Click **OK**.

You can also display the **Insert Function** dialog box by clicking the **Insert Function** tool f_x to the left of the Formula bar.

Insert Function dialog box

1 Describe what you are trying to do and click **Go**.

Or

- Select a function category, and then select a function.
2 Once you've found the function, select it and click **OK**.

- If the function you want has been used recently, it will be listed in the *Most Recently Used* list. If you're not sure what category the function you require is in, select *All* (every function is listed here, in alphabetical order). Minimum, Maximum, Average and Count can be found in the *Statistical* category.

3 Enter the range you want the function to operate on – either drag over the range, or type the cell addresses (minimize the **Function Argument** dialog box – click 🔙 on the right of the function argument field – so you can see your worksheet).

4 Restore the **Function Argument** dialog box – click 🔲 on the right of the function argument field.

5 Click **OK**.

In this example statistical functions were used to display:

- The **lowest** result in each exam (minimum)
- The **highest** result in each exam (maximum)
- The **average** mark for each subject (average)
- The **number** of students (count).

	A	B	C	D	E	F
1	Exam Results					
2						
3	Firstname	Surname	Maths	English	Computing	
4	Alison	Anderson	60%	45%	80%	
5	Bill	Andrews	50%	88%	59%	
6	Gavin	Blair	63%	56%	72%	
7	Jill	Blair	50%	80%	76%	
8	Julie	Collins	74%	68%	78%	
9	Paul	Dunsire	30%	60%	95%	
10	Anne	Peterson	70%	68%	74%	
11						
12	Lowest Mark		30%	45%	59%	
13	Highest Mark		74%	88%	95%	
14	Average Mark		57%	66%	76%	
15						
16	Number of students		7			
17						

CountA

The **Count** function will count how many *numeric* entries are in a range of cells.

If you wish to count the number of entries in a range of cells, regardless of whether the entry is numeric or non-numeric, use the **CountA** function e.g. =CountA(A2:A12).

Round

The Round function is used to specify the number or decimal places that you want a value in a cell displayed to, e.g. =Round(C4,2) entered in C5 would display (in C5) the value in cell C4 to a accuracy of 2 decimal places.

10	
23.4	
30	
32.444	

=ROUND(SUM(C7:C11),2)

ROUND(number, num_digits)

You can also use the Round function to control the accuracy of the current cell as here. The sum of (C7:C11) will be displayed with an accuracy of 2 decimal places.

5.14 View formula

When setting up your worksheet, it is sometimes useful to display and print the formulas that you have entered into the cells.

To toggle the display of the formulas:

1 Open the **Tools** menu and select **Options...**

2 Select the **View** tab.

3 Select (to show formulas) or deselect (to hide formulas) the *Formulas* checkbox.

4 Click **OK**.

Microsoft Excel - TY Examples.xls

File Edit View Insert Format Tools Data Window Help   Type a

100%   10   B I U

	A	B	C	D	E
1	**Exam Results**				
2					
3	**Firstname**	**Surname**	**Maths**	**English**	**Computing**
4	Alison	Anderson	0.6	0.45	0.8
5	Bill	Andrews	0.5	0.88	0.59
6	Gavin	Blair	0.63	0.56	0.72
7	Jill	Blair	0.5	0.8	0.76
8	Julie	Collins	0.74	0.68	0.78
9	Paul	Dunsire	0.3	0.6	0.95
10	Anne	Peterson	0.7	0.68	0.74
11					
12	**Lowest Mark**		=MIN(C4:C10)	=MIN(D4:D10)	=MIN(E4:E10)
13	**Highest Mark**		=MAX(C4:C10)	=MAX(D4:D10)	=MAX(E4:E10)
14	**Average Mark**		=AVERAGE(C4:C10)	=AVERAGE(D4:D10)	=AVERAGE(E4:E10)
15					
16	**Number of students**		=COUNT(C4:C10)		
17					

♦ Or use the shortcut **[Ctrl]–[l]** (to the left of **[1]**).

You may need to adjust the column widths to display the whole formula or function in some columns.

♦ You can print a copy of your worksheet out with the formulas displayed – you may find it useful for reference purposes.

5.15 Sort

The data in a worksheet can be sorted into ascending or descending order. A simple sort is where the data is sorted using the entries in one column only. You can also have more complex sorts, where you can sort on up to three columns at a time.

To perform a simple sort:

1 Select any cell in the column you want to base your sort on.

2 Click the Sort Ascending or Sort Descending tool on the Standard toolbar.

To perform a multi-level sort:

1 Select any cell within the group of cells you want sorted.

2 Open the **Data** menu and choose **Sort...**

3 Select the main sort field from the **Sort by** list.

4 Click **Ascending** or **Descending**.

5 Select the second level sort field from the first **Then by** list, and set its sort order.

6 If necessary, set the third level sort options.

7 Click **OK**.

♦ By default, Excel assumes your list has a Header row. This is the row that normally contains the column labels or field names. If your list doesn't have one, i.e. you want to include the first row in the sort, select the **No header row** option.

5.16 IF function

The IF function is used to return one value if the condition you specify is True, and another value if the condition is False. The values returned can be text, numbers, or the result of a formula or function.

For example, you might be entering student end-of-term exam results into your worksheet. If a student has 50% or more in the exam, a pass will be awarded, if less than 50% is achieved, the result is a fail.

Comparison operators

This example uses a *comparison* operator to check if the total mark is greater than or equal to 50. The operators include:

=	equal to	<>	not equal to
>	greater than	>=	greater than or equal to
<	less than	<=	less than or equal to

+ Enter the data below into a new worksheet.

	A	B	C	D	E
1	END OF TERM EXAM RESULTS				
2					
3	Firstname	Surname	Total Mark	Result	
4	Andrew	Borthwick	75		
5	Gill	McLaren	57		
6	Amanda	Mitchell	76		
7	Alison	Peterson	66		
8	Ann	Shaw	42		
9	Peter	Shaw	63		
10	Clare	Stephen	83		
11	Kim	Stephen	79		
12	Gordon	Williamson	39		
13	Jack	Williamson	77		
14					

+ To return a 'Pass' or 'Fail' message in the *Result* column, we need to enter the IF function.

To enter the function:

1 Select the first cell in the *Result* column.

2 Press = to start the function.

3 Display the function list at the extreme left of the Formula bar row (the name box changes to this when you press =) – click the drop-down arrow to display the list.

4 Select the IF function from the list.

Or

- If the function you require isn't in the list, click **More Functions** to open the Function Arguments dialog box and locate the IF function from there (in the Logical category).

5 Enter the condition in the **Logical test** field, e.g. C4>=50.

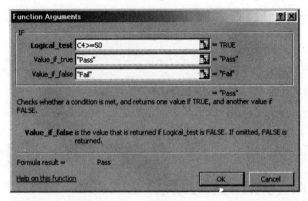

6 Specify the value if the condition if found to be true. You don't need to type quotes – Excel enters them automatically.

7 Specify the value if the condition is found to be false.

8 Click **OK**.

- AutoFill the formula down through the *Result* column. 'Pass' will appear where the condition is true, 'Fail' where it is false.

With the formulas displayed, the worksheet looks like the illustration below.

	A	B	C	D	E
1	**END OF 1**				
2					
3	**Firstname**	**Surname**	**Total Mark**	**Result**	
4	Andrew	Borthwick	75	=IF(C4>=50,"Pass","Fail")	
5	Gill	McLaren	57	=IF(C5>=50,"Pass","Fail")	
6	Amanda	Mitchell	76	=IF(C6>=50,"Pass","Fail")	
7	Alison	Peterson	66	=IF(C7>=50,"Pass","Fail")	
8	Ann	Shaw	42	=IF(C8>=50,"Pass","Fail")	
9	Peter	Shaw	63	=IF(C9>=50,"Pass","Fail")	
10	Clare	Stephen	83	=IF(C10>=50,"Pass","Fail")	
11	Kim	Stephen	79	=IF(C11>=50,"Pass","Fail")	
12	Gordon	Williamson	39	=IF(C12>=50,"Pass","Fail")	
13	Jack	Williamson	77	=IF(C13>=50,"Pass","Fail")	
14					

5.17 Relative and absolute addresses

You have already noticed that when you AutoFill or copy a formula, the cell addresses used in it change automatically, relative to the position that you copy them to. By default, the cell addresses used in formulas are what we call *relative addresses*.

There will be times when you use a cell address in a formula, want to copy it down some rows or across some columns, but don't want the address to change relative to its new position.

In this example, we are going to calculate the amount of foreign currency we would get for our holiday spending money (£150). We are going to calculate its value in Euros, Dollars, Kroon (Estonia) and Rupees (India).

• You could find the current exchange rates on the Internet.

The formula required in cell C4 is =B4*C1.

When the formula is copied, we want B4 to become B5 (for dollars), B6 (for kroon) and B7 (for rupees).

We *don't* want C1 (our spending money in £), to change at all.

	A	B	C
1	**Spending money (£)**		150
2			
3		Exchange rate to the £	Value of spending money
4	Euros	1.38754	
5	Dollars	1.6385	
6	Estonian Kroon	21.715	
7	Indian Rupee	76.89808	
8			

To stop the cell address changing when we copy it, we must make it *absolute*. An absolute address will not change when the formula containing it is copied or moved.

• Enter a $ sign in front of each co-ordinate you do not want to change.

You can type the $ sign, or use [F4].

To create absolute addresses in a formula:

1 Select the cell that contains the formula (C4 in this example) – the formula appears in the Formula bar.

2 Click in the Formula bar.

3 Place the insertion point to the *right* of the cell address you want to make absolute (C1).

4 Press [F4] to change the nature of the address. Each time you press [F4] it moves through the absolute addressing options.

$C$1   neither co-ordinate will change

C$1   the column will change if you copy the formula across columns

$C1   the row will change if you copy down rows

C1   both co-ordinates will change relative to its new position.

Your final worksheet should look similar to the one below. The first picture displays the formulas (you may have different cell addresses if you have used different rows and columns for your data), the second one shows the results.

	A	B	C
1	**Spending mo**		**150**
2			
3		Exchange rate to the £	Value of spending money
4	Euros	1.38754	=$C$1*B4
5	Dollars	1.6385	=$C$1*B5
6	Estonian Kroon	21.715	=$C$1*B6
7	Indian Rupee	76.89808	=$C$1*B7
8			

	A	B	C	D
1	**Spending money (£)**		**150**	
2				
3		Exchange rate to the £	Value of spending money	
4	Euros	1.38754	€ 208.13	
5	Dollars	1.6385	$245.78	
6	Estonian Kroon	21.715	3,257.25 kr	
7	Indian Rupee	76.89808	INR 11,534.71	
8				

The currency formats are found in the Format Cells dialog box. Select the Number tab, then the Currency category. Scroll through the Symbol list until you find the symbol required.

Common error messages

Error	Common Reason	Solution
#######	Column not wide enough	Adjust column width
Value!	A value used in the formula is of the wrong data type, e.g. text	Put a number in the cell, or amend the cell address
#DIV/0!	You are dividing by a cell that is empty or contains 0	Enter a value in the cell, or amend the cell address
#REF!	The cell referenced has been deleted	Replace #REF! In the formula with a valid cell address

Full details of error messages, possible causes and solutions, are available in the online Help.

5.18 Preview, Page Setup and Print

It is very important that the worksheet that you print and distribute is accurate and well presented. You must check the accuracy of the spreadsheet carefully, e.g. spell check the file, check that the data and formulas are correct.

In addition to this, there are several options that you can use to ensure that your worksheet is displayed effectively.

Print Preview

At some stage you will want to print your file. Before sending a worksheet to print, it's a good idea to *preview* it.

You cannot edit an Excel worksheet in Print Preview. If you want to change something when you see the preview:

1 Click the **Close** tool on the Print Preview toolbar to return to your worksheet.

2 Edit the worksheet as required.

3 Preview again to see how it looks.

Page Setup

The Page Setup dialog box can be used to change the orientation, paper size, margins and other aspects of the printed layout.

Pages are usually printed portrait (rather than landscape).

To change the orientation:

1 From a worksheet, open the **File** menu and choose **Page Setup**.

Or

* If you are in Print Preview, click the **Setup...** button on the Print Preview toolbar to open the **Page Setup** dialog box.

2 Select the **Page** tab.

3 Choose an Orientation option – portrait or landscape.

4 Click **OK**.

The default paper size used for printing is A4. You can select an alternative page size if necessary.

To change the paper size:

1 Open the **Page Setup** dialog box and select the **Page** tab.

2 Choose the paper size from the **Paper size** list.

3 Click **OK**.

To change the margins:

1 Open the **Page Setup** dialog box and select the **Margins** tab.

2 Specify the margins you want to use.

3 Click **OK**.

If your sheet is more than a page in size, you can specify how many pages to print it on with the Scaling option. You can also specify whether to print *down then across* or *across then down*.

To change the scaling:

1 Open the **Page Setup** dialog box and select the **Page** tab.

2 In the **Scaling** options, specify the number of pages wide and the number of pages tall you want your worksheet to fit on.

3 Click **OK**.

- This option is particularly useful if the last page of your worksheet contains only a small amount of data. You can specify that the worksheet print on one page less than it really needs – Excel will scale it down to fit onto that number of pages.

To specify the order of printing:

1 Open the **Page Setup** dialog box and select the **Sheet** tab.

2 In the **Page order** options, select the order required.

3 Click **OK**.

Page breaks

If your worksheet runs to more than one page, Excel will divide it into pages by inserting automatic page breaks. Exactly where the page breaks appear depends on the paper size, margin settings and scaling options. You can set your own page breaks.

To insert a horizontal page break:

1 Select the row *below* where you want the page break.

2 Open the **Insert** menu and click **Page Break**.

To insert a vertical page break:

1 Select the column to the *right* of where you want the page break.

2 Open the **Insert** menu and click **Page Break**.

To move a page break:

1 Open the **View** menu and click **Page Break Preview**.

- The first time you go into Page Break Preview a prompt will tell you how to move the breaks – if you don't want this prompt to appear again, select the checkbox and click **OK**.

2 Drag the page break to its new position.

To insert a horizontal and vertical page break at the same time:

1 Select the cell immediately below and to the right of where you want to start a new page.

2 Open the **Insert** menu and click **Page Break**.

To remove a page break:

1 Open the **View** menu and click **Page Break Preview**.

2 Right-click on a cell below a horizontal page break.

Or

◆ Right-click on a cell to the right of the vertical page break.

3 Click **Remove Page Break** on the shortcut menu.

4 Open the **View** menu and click **Normal** to return to your worksheet.

Repeat heading rows and columns

If you have a big spreadsheet, with headings that you would like repeated on each page printed, you can use the Repeat options.

1 Display the **Page Setup** dialog box and select the **Sheet** tab.

2 In the **Print Titles** area, click in the **Rows to repeat at top** field and enter the range of rows, e.g. 1:3, or in the **Columns to repeat at left** and enter the column letters, e.g. A:B.

Or

3 Drag over the range required.

4 Click **OK**.

Headers and footers

Headers and footers display information at the top or bottom of every page that prints out for your worksheet. They are useful for page numbers, your name, the date that the worksheet is printed, the worksheet name, the workbook name – or any other information that you would like to appear in them.

To add a header and/or footer to your pages:

1 Open the **Page Setup** dialog box.

2 Select the **Header/Footer** tab.

3 Choose a header or footer from the list of options available.

4 Click **OK**.

Gridlines, row and column headings

When you print your worksheet out, the gridlines, row and column headings do not print. This is usually how you would want

it, but there may be times when it is useful to print them out –
for example, when printing out the formulas.

1 Display the **Page Setup** and select the **Sheet** tab.
2 In the **Print** options, select the **Gridlines** and/or **Row and column headings** checkboxes as required.
3 Click **OK**.

Print

When you are happy with the preview, you can send it to print.

♦ Click the **Print** button on the Standard toolbar to print one
copy of the worksheet.

Or

1 Select **Print** from the **File** menu (or click **Print…** on the **Print Preview** toolbar).
2 Complete the **Print** dialog box as required – specify the **Print range**, **Copies** and **Print what** options as required.
3 Click **OK**.

You can print just a part of your worksheet, if you like.

To print part of your worksheet:

1 Select the range of cells you want to print.
2 Open the **File** menu and choose **Print…**
3 Select **Selection** from the **Print what** options.
4 Click **OK**.

5.19 Charts

Excel can create charts – bar graphs, line graphs, pie charts,
scatter diagrams, etc. – from the data in your worksheet.

You can create your chart as an object on the same worksheet as
the data on which it is built, or on a separate chart sheet.

♦ Data that you want to chart should *ideally* be in cells that are
adjacent to each other. If the data has blank rows or columns
within it, remove these before you try to chart the data.

	A	B	C	D	E	F	G
1	**BOOKSHOP SALE**						
2							
3	Title	Rec Retail Price	Sale Price	Saving	No in Stock	Value of Stock	
4	Cats	£ 12.00	£ 4.80	£ 7.20	4	£ 19.20	
5	Wine tasting holidays	£ 14.00	£ 5.60	£ 8.40	6	£ 33.60	
6	Canal boat holidays	£ 10.00	£ 4.00	£ 6.00	12	£ 48.00	
7	Italian Family Cookbook	£ 14.50	£ 5.80	£ 8.70	8	£ 46.40	
8							
9						£147.20	
10							

To chart data that is not in adjacent cells:

1 Select the first group of cells you want to chart.

2 Hold down [Ctrl] while you click and drag over the other groups you want to include in your chart.

♦ When the non-adjacent cells are selected, the selected areas *must* be able to combine to form a rectangle.

Chart Wizard

The Chart Wizard is used to step you through the process of setting up your chart.

To create a chart:

1 Select the data to chart – including the column headings and row labels.

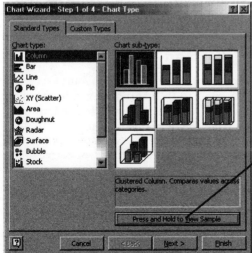

Click to see what your data would look like in your chosen chart type

2 Click the **Chart Wizard** tool 📖 on the Standard toolbar.

3 At step 1 of the Chart Wizard, select the **Chart type**.

4 Once you've decided on a type, click **Next**.

5 At step 2, on the **Data Range** tab, check the data range selected, decide whether you want to display the data series in rows or columns (try both and decide which you prefer). Click **Next**.

6 At step 3, explore the **Chart Options** tab and set the options. You can add chart or axis titles here (**Titles** tab), or reposition the Legend (**Legend** tab). Click **Next** to move on.

7 Finally, decide where the chart should be located – in your worksheet, or on a separate chart sheet, and click **Finish**.

♦ Once a chart has been created, changes made to the data on which the chart is based, will automatically be reflected in the chart. This happens regardless of whether the chart is an object in your worksheet, or on a separate chart sheet.

A chart in your worksheet

The Chart toolbar should be displayed when the chart in your worksheet is selected.

♦ If the chart is selected, there will be *handles* in each corner and along each side.

♦ If you click on the worksheet area, the chart is deselected, and the Chart toolbar disappears.

♦ To select the chart again, click on it once.

Move, resize and delete chart

If you want to move, resize or delete a chart you must first select the *chart area* – either point to the chart area within the chart and click (a prompt will tell you what the mouse is pointing at) or choose **Chart Area** from the object list on the Chart toolbar.

To move the chart:

1 Select the chart area.

2 Drag the chart to its new position.

To resize the chart:

1 Select the chart.

2 Drag a handle on the edge of the chart to change its size.

To delete the chart:

1 Select the chart.

2 Press [Delete].

A chart on a separate sheet

If you opt to locate your chart in a new sheet, it will be displayed on a sheet called *Chart1* (or *Chart2* or *Chart3* for later charts). This is inserted to the left of the sheet that its data is on.

You can rename the *Chart1* sheet name to something more meaningful, move the sheet to another location in your workbook, or delete it if you decide you don't need it any more.

The Chart toolbar should be displayed when the Chart sheet is selected. You can use the Chart toolbar, or the Format or Chart menu to modify the chart as required.

Chart menu

The Chart menu appears when you have a chart selected. Take a look at its options and their dialog boxes.

- **Chart Type...** displays the dialog box from Step 1 of the Wizard. You access all the chart types and sub-types here.

- **Source Data...** displays the dialog box from Step 2 of the Wizard. Use this to edit the data range.

- **Chart Options...** displays the dialog box from Step 3. You can add titles, edit the legend, gridlines, etc. from here.

- **Location...** displays the dialog box from Step 4. You can change the location of the selected chart from here – move it to another sheet, or put it on a Chart sheet.

Chart objects

Each area of a chart is an object – you have a chart area object, plot area object, category axis object, legend object, etc.

The chart must be selected (if it is an object in your workbook) before you can select the individual objects within it.

To select a chart object:

- Choose the object from the Chart Objects list.

Or

- Click on the object you want to select.

Chart object

Format

Formatting chart objects

You can change the formatting of each object in your chart, e.g. the colours in a bar chart, or the position of the legend.

To format an object in your chart:

* Select the object, e.g. the legend, a series of data, the title.
* Use the italic, bold, underline, font, font size, fill, text colour, etc. tools on the Formatting toolbar.

Or

* Double-click the chart object you want to format.

To change the chart type

If your chart doesn't look the way you expected, and you think a different chart type would be better, you can change the chart type at any time.

To change the chart type:

1 Click the drop-down arrow to the right of the **Chart Type** tool on the Chart toolbar.

2 Select the type of chart required.

Printing charts

You can print your chart with or without the data on which it is based. To print a chart that is an object within your worksheet you have several options. I suggest you do a Print Preview before you actually print, just to check it looks okay.

To get a print out of the chart only:

* Select the chart on the worksheet, then print.

To print out all of the data on the worksheet and the chart:

* Print the worksheet as normal (do not select the chart first).

To get the chart and its data only:

1 Select the chart.

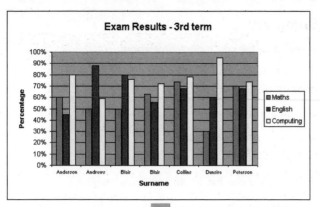

2 Click the **Data Table** tool 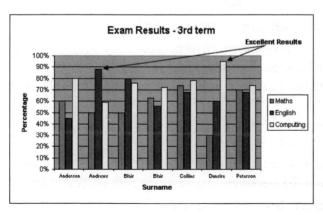 on the Chart toolbar to display the data table for the chart.

3 Print out with the chart selected.

To print a chart that is on a separate Chart sheet:

1 Select the Chart sheet.

2 Print as usual.

♦ If you also want to print out the data on which the chart is based, display the Data Table before you print.

You can use the drawing tools to create different effects on your worksheet data and charts. If you create charts, try using an arrow and a text box to add emphasis to it! (See section 3.11.)

Summary

In this chapter you have learnt about:

* Worksheets and workbooks
* Spreadsheet jargon
* Moving around your sheet
* Selection techniques
* Entering text and data into a worksheet
* Adjusting column widths and row heights
* Formatting options that are specific to spreadsheets
* Freezing headings
* Split screen
* Entering formulas using the operators +, -, * and /
* AutoFill
* Sum and AutoSum
* Statistical functions – Average, Minimum, Maximum, Count, CountA
* The Round function
* Sorting your data
* The IF function
* Absolute and relative addressing
* Previewing and printing
* Creating and manipulating charts.

06
databases

In this chapter you will learn

- about Access and databases
- how to create tables
- how to enter and edit data
- how to extract records
- how to produce reports

6.1 Planning and design

A simple database could be used to store names and addresses (e.g. your Christmas card list) or the details of your CD collection; a more complex one could organize the data you need to run your company (supplier, customer, stock, order details, etc.).

In a simple database, it may be feasible to store all the information in one table – as you could with a Christmas card list. Other databases are more complex with several tables, e.g. a company database with details of customers, staff and suppliers.

Some database terminology may be unfamiliar to you. Below are brief definitions of the terms you are likely to encounter.

Term	Definition
Table	The data on one topic is stored in a table. A simple database may have only one table. More complex databases may consist of several tables.
Record	The data for a single item in your table, e.g. the details relating to one book in a Library table.
Field	A piece of data within a record, e.g. in a book's record, things like ISBN, title or author.
Relationship	Links the detail in one table to the detail in another table, e.g. through the ISBN.
Join	The process of linking tables or queries.
Data definition	The process of defining what data will be stored, specifying the field's type (number, text, etc.), size and how it is related to data in other tables.
Data manipulation	Work done on a database, e.g. sorting it into an order, extracting records from tables, or listing detail from several tables into one report.
Data	Raw facts, e.g. Book price = £20.00, Publisher = Hodder & Stoughton, No of copies = 5
Information	Processed data, e.g. The value of books from Hodder & Stoughton is £100.

Example database

In this chapter we will set up a database that could be used to record details of the books in a library. It will hold these details:

- Book title, author, price, year published
- Publisher name, address and other contact details

Schematic diagram of a database

LIBRARY DATABASE

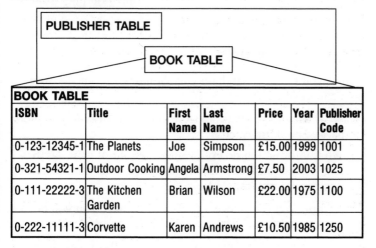

BOOK TABLE						
ISBN	**Title**	**First Name**	**Last Name**	**Price**	**Year**	**Publisher Code**
0-123-12345-1	The Planets	Joe	Simpson	£15.00	1999	1001
0-321-54321-1	Outdoor Cooking	Angela	Armstrong	£7.50	2003	1025
0-111-22222-3	The Kitchen Garden	Brian	Wilson	£22.00	1975	1100
0-222-11111-3	Corvette	Karen	Andrews	£10.50	1985	1250

The diagram above illustrates our database.

- Each *record* in a table is presented in a row.
- Each *field* in a record is in a column.
- Each field has a *field name* at the top of the column.

The database that we create in this chapter will illustrate some of the benefits of using databases. In real life there are some very large-scale databases in regular use (and your details could be in many of them). Airline booking systems, government records, bank account records, hospital patient details, pupil/students record systems are just a few examples.

Access objects

An Access database consists of *objects* that can be used to input, display, interrogate, print and automate your work. These are listed in the Database window. The ones we will be using are:

- **Tables** – the most important objects in your database. Tables hold data and are used for data entry and edit. They display data in a datasheet (it looks like a worksheet in Excel).

- **Queries** – used to locate specific records in your tables using various criteria, e.g. overdue books or all science fiction books.

- **Forms** – used to provide an alternative and more 'user friendly' front end to your tables for entering and editing records.

- **Reports** – used to produce various printed outputs from the data in your database.

Preparing your data

Before you set up a database you should work out the answers to a couple of questions:

- What data do you want to store in the database? (e.g. authors' names, book titles, etc.)

- What information do you want to get out of your database? (e.g. a list of all books that are overdue, a list of all books by a particular author, etc.)

If you work out the answers to these questions, you will be in a position to start working out what fields you need.

If you are setting up names, you would probably break the name into three fields – Title, First name (or Initials) and Last name. This way you can sort the file into Last name order, or search for someone using the First name and Last name.

If you are storing addresses, you would probably want separate fields for Street, Town/City, Region, Postcode and/or Country. You can then sort your records into order on any field, or locate records by specifying search criteria. For example, using Street and Town/City fields, you could search for details of people who live in St John's Street, Stirling rather than St John's Street, Dundee.

When planning your database, take a small sample of the data you wish to store and examine it carefully. This will help you confirm what fields will be required.

You must also decide how much space is required for each field. The space you allocate must be long enough to accommodate the longest item that might go there. How long is the longest last name you want to store? If in doubt, take a sample of some typical names (Anderson, Johnston, Mackenzie, Harvey-Jones?) and add a few more characters to the longest one to be sure.

Primary Key

Most records will have a unique identifier – a field that holds different information in every record in your table. In our database, each book would have an ISBN number and this would be different for each book. The field that must be unique in each record is set as the Primary Key. You cannot enter duplicate information into a primary key field – Access will not allow it.

Try to group your fields into tables with a view to minimizing the duplication of data in your database.

There are several benefits to this approach:

• Each set of details is stored (and therefore typed in) only once.

• The tables are smaller than they otherwise might have been.

• As you don't have much duplication of data, the database is easier to maintain and keep up to date.

It is very important that you spend time organizing and structuring your data before you start to computerize it – it'll save you a lot of time and frustration in the long run!

Database operational issues

In large institutions, e.g. banks and government departments, creating and managing the databases is a very important and specialist function. Systems analysts, data analysts and database administrators are some of the specialists that will be involved in the creation and maintenance of large database systems.

Data entry and the updating of data will be the responsibility of the users, e.g. office administrators, management assistants, sales staff, etc. They will enter and edit the data, run the queries and produce the reports required by managers and clients.

Users will not necessarily be given access to all areas of a database – they will be granted access to whatever areas they need to perform their job. The database administrator is the person that gives users the appropriate rights so that they can access the information they require. It is also the database administrator who is responsible for recovery of the database system if there is a system crash.

6.2 Starting Access

When you start Access, the Access screen will appear with the Getting Started task pane on the right.

To create our Library database:

- Click **Create a new file...** on the Getting Started task pane.

Or

If you are in Access, but have not created the database, do so now:

- Click the **New** tool on the **Database** toolbar, then click **Blank Database** on the New file task pane.

You arrive at the **File New Database** dialog box.

Where do you want to store your database? *My Documents* is the default – select the folder or drive in the **Save in** field.

As with all Microsoft packages, a temporary filename is suggested – in Access these follow the pattern *db1*, *db2*, *db3*. You need to replace this with a name that reflects the contents of your database.

The example database used here is one that may help in the running of a library. Name your database *Library*.

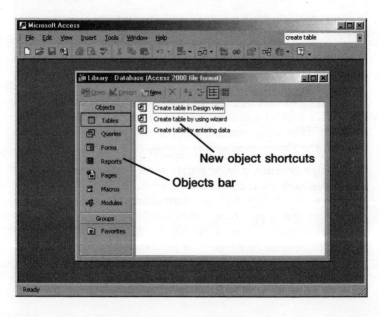

- Once you have named the database click the **Create** button.

This takes you through into Access, with your Library database window displayed.

6.3 Field data types and properties

Data types

There are 10 different data types to choose from when setting up your tables. Most of your fields will probably be Text, with a few of the others used in each table depending on the type of data. These are the data types that you will use most often.

Data type	Usage	Size	Notes
Text	Alphanumeric data	up to 255 bytes	Default data type
Number	Numeric data	1,2,4 or 8 bytes	
Date/Time	Dates and times	8 bytes	Values for the years 100 through to 9999
Currency	Monetary data	8 bytes	Accurate to 4 decimal places and 15 digits to the left of the decimal separator
AutoNumber	Unique long integer created by Access	4 bytes	Cannot be updated Useful for primary keys
Yes/No	Boolean data	1 bit	Yes and No values, and fields that contain 1 of 2 values On/Off, True/False

Properties

You can customize each field by specifying different properties. These vary depending on the data type. The ones most commonly used are listed below.

Property	Data type	Notes
Field Size	Text and Number Number field sizes are: Byte (single byte) Integer (2-byte) Long Integer (4-byte) Single (4-byte) Double (8-byte)	Text from 1 to 255 characters Values: 0 to 255 -32,768 to +32,767 -2,147,483,647 to 2,147,483,647 -3.4 x 1038 to 3.4 x 1038 -1.797 x 10308 to +1.797 x 10308
Format		Options depend on the data type
Decimal places	Number and Currency	Auto (displays 2 d.p. for most formats) or Fixed: 0 to 15 d.p.
Caption		For display on forms and reports
Default Value	All except Memo, OLE Object and AutoNumber	
Validation Rule		Used to test that suitable data is entered
Validation Text		The message to appear on screen when a validation rule is not met
Required		Set to Yes if data must be entered
Indexed	Text, Number, Currency, Date/Time and AutoNumber types	Indexing speeds up access to its data – fields that will be sorted or queried on should be indexed

6.4 Creating a new table

• Double click 🗐 Create table in Design view .

Or

1 Select **Tables** on the **Objects** bar.

2 Click **New** 🔚New on the Database window toolbar.

3 Select **Design View**.

4 Click **OK**.

In the table design you identify the fields required, their data types and any other properties that are important. We will set up two table designs: the *Books* and *Publisher* tables.

Define fields in the upper pane …

⊞ Table1 : Table			
Field Name	Data Type	Description	
ISBN	Text	Primary Key	
Title	Text		
Classification|	Text		
Year Published	Text		
PublisherID	Text	Link to Publisher table	
AuthorID	Text	Link to Author table	
Cover	Text		
Price	Currency		

Field Properties

General | Lookup

Field Size	20
Format	
Input Mask	
Caption	
Default Value	"Fiction"
Validation Rule	
Validation Text	
Required	No
Allow Zero Length	Yes
Indexed	Yes (Duplicates OK)
Unicode Compression	Yes
IME Mode	No Control
IME Sentence Mode	None

…and properties in the lower pane

Defining the table structure

The *Books* table will contain the fields listed below.

Field name	Data type	Properties
ISBN	Text	Primary Key, Field Size = 20
Title	Text	Field Size = 35, Indexed (Duplicates OK)
Classification	Text	Field Size = 20, Default Value = Fiction, Indexed (Duplicates OK)
Year published	Text	Field Size = 4
Publisher ID	Text	Field Size = 6
Author Firstname	Text	Field Size = 15
Author Surname	Text	Field Size = 15
Cover	Text	Field Size = 12, Default Value = Paperback
Price	Currency	Validation Rule <100 No book cost over £100

♦ The Publisher ID field will be used to link to the *Publisher* table, where the contact details of each publisher will be held. This means that if we have several books from one publisher, we can store the contact details *once* in the Publisher table – reducing duplication of data.

Primary Key/Foreign Key

A Primary Key field is the one that is the unique identifier in each table. In these tables, the Primary Key in the *Books* table is the ISBN (the International Standard Book Number, which is different for every book that is publshed) and in the *Publisher* table it is the Publisher ID.

The Publisher ID appears in the *Books* table. Although an ID field, it is not the Primary Key in this table – it is a Foreign Key. A Foreign Key refers to a Primary Key in another table.

In the *Books* table, the first field is the ISBN.

1 In the Field Name column, key in the field name – 'ISBN'.

2 Press [**Tab**] to move along to the Data Type column and set this to *Text* (the default data type).

◆ The default size for a Text field is 50 characters. This is more than is required for an ISBN and it could be reduced to 20.

3 Press [**F6**] to move to the lower pane (or click with the mouse) and change the field size from 50 to 20, then press [**F6**] to return to the upper pane.

4 Press [**Tab**] to move along to the Description column and enter a field description if you wish.

◆ The Description is optional – anything typed here will appear on the Status bar (as a prompt to the operator) during data entry to that field.

5 To set Primary Key status, click the Primary Key tool when the insertion point is in the ISBN row in the top pane.

Note that the Index property is automatically set to *Yes (No Duplicates)* when a field is given Primary Key status.

Enter the Title details in the second row of the upper pane.

1 In the Field Name column, key in the field name – 'Title'.

2 Press [**Tab**] to move to the Data Type column and select Text.

3 Set the field size to 35.

4 Set the Indexed property to *Yes (Duplicates OK)*.

Enter the remaining fields following the suggestions in the table.

Save and close the Table Design window

1 Click **Save** on the Table Design toolbar.

2 Give your table a suitable name, e.g. *Books*.

3 Click **OK**.

4 Close the Table Design window.

Save As dialog box showing Table Name: Books, with OK and Cancel buttons.

Your new table will be listed in the Database window.

Setting up the Publisher table

1 Create a new table as above.

2 Set up the structure for this table, following the suggestions.

Field name	Data type	Properties	Notes
Publisher ID	Text	Field Size = 6	Primary Key
Company Name	Text	Field Size = 35	Indexed (Duplicates OK)
Address	Text	Field Size = 30	
Town	Text	Field Size = 20	Indexed (Duplicates OK), Default Value = London
Postcode	Text	Field Size = 10	
Telephone No	Text	Field Size = 20	
Email	Text	Field Size = 40	

3 Save and close the table.

♦ Close the Table Design window.

6.5 Relationships

We now have to set up the relationships between these tables.

1 Click the **Relationships** tool on the Database toolbar at the Database window. The Relationships window opens.

♦ The Show Table window should also be displayed – if it isn't click the **Show Table** tool to display a list of the tables.

2 Select the table(s) to add to the Relationships window and click **Add**.

3 Click **Close** once you have added your tables.

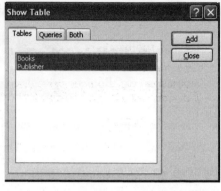

We need to create a relationship between the *Books* and *Publisher* tables using the Publisher ID. With the tables related, we will be able to pull information from more than one table at a time if necessary.

Relationship type

One-to-many – one of the related fields is a Primary Key or has a unique index. This is the most common type of relationship. In our example a Publisher in the *Publisher* table can have many matching records in the *Books* table – a one-to-many relationship.

One-to-one – both the related fields are Primary Keys or contain unique indexes. Each record in the first table can have only one matching record in the second, and vice versa. One-to-one relationships are used to divide a table that has many fields, or to isolate fields for security reasons. This type of relationship may be used when storing personnel data where you could have general information in one table, e.g. name, address, job title, and confidential information in another, e.g. salary, bank details, etc.

Referential integrity

These are the rules that are followed to preserve the defined relationships between tables when you enter or delete records. If you enforce referential integrity, Access prevents you from:

• Adding records to a related table when there is no associated record in the primary table.

• Changing values in the primary table that would result in orphan (unconnected) records in a related table.

- Deleting records from the primary table when there are matching related records in a related table.

To create a relationship:

1 Click on the field you wish to relate to another table.

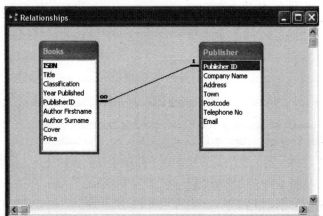

2 Drag the field and drop it onto the field you wish to link it to in the other table.

3 At the **Edit Relationships** dialog box, select **Referential Integrity** (if desired) and click **Create** to establish the relationship.

4 Click **OK**.

The lines between the fields linking the tables are called *join lines*.

To delete an existing relationship:

1 Click on the join line you wish to remove to select it.

2 Press **[Delete]** and respond to the prompt as required.

- Save the changes made to the Relationship window if you wish to keep them and close the window when you have done.

6.6 Entering data in Datasheet view

You should have the Library database open. The two tables will be listed in the Tables area of the Database window.

Data entry is generally easy. You simply open the table and key in the data – using [Tab] or the mouse to move from field to field. As you are keying in the data, look out for these features.

- To open a table in Datasheet view, double-click on its name, or select the table in the **Tables** list and click **Open**.

In Datasheet view, a table looks similar to a spreadsheet layout – each record is presented in a row and each field is in a column.

- To move forward through the fields press [**Tab**].
- To move backward through the fields press [**Shift**]-[**Tab**].

Or

- Click in the field you want to move to using the mouse.

For the *Publisher* table, enter the records shown on page 193.

You will notice that the Town field is completed automatically with London – our default value. Make up another 6 records.

- Close the table when you've finished. You don't need to save your data – Access does this automatically.

For the *Books* table, enter details of the books that you have in your library, or use the data given on page 193. Add another 10, using the same classifications.

- Close the table when you've finished.

Note: if you have enforced referential integrity, you must complete the table at the *one* side of the relationship before entering the related records at the *many* side.

Editing data in Datasheet view

At the bottom left of the table window, you will find a set of navigation buttons that you can use to move through your table in Datasheet view, instead of using [Tab] or the mouse.

- The record number field tells you which record the insertion point is currently in, and to the right of this you will find the total number of records in your table.

Editing the field contents

If you spot an error in Datasheet view, you must position the insertion point within the field you wish to edit, and make whatever changes are required.

Publisher Table

Pub ID	Company Name	Address	Town	Postcode	Telephone No	Email
P1	Hodder & Stoughton	338 Euston Road	London	NW1 3BH	0171 111 2222	hodinfo@hotmail.com
P2	Westward Lock Ltd	18 Clifftop Street	London	W1X 1RB		Gill.A@yahoo.com
P3	Alice Publications	4 High Street	Oxford	OX1 2QQ		a.smith@hotmail.com
P4	Puffin Books	3 West Row	London	NW2 3SL	0181 222 3333	

Books Table

ISBN	Title	Classification	Year published	Publisher ID	Author First name	Author Last name	Cover	Price
1-12345-123	The Snow Storm	Fiction	1985	P2	Gill	Peterson	Paperback	£7.99
2-54321-321	Indian Highlights	Travel	1997	P3	Andrew	Borthwick	Paperback	£9.99
3-13243-312	Elm Grove	Children's	1996	P2	Clare	Adams	Paperback	£6.99
4-53423-222	Africa Trekker	Travel	1994	P1	Andrew	Borthwick	Paperback	£6.99
5-11111-222	The Lying Stone	Fiction	1954	P4	Kim	Simpson	Hardback	£16.99

You can use the scroll bars (horizontal and vertical), or the navigation buttons to locate the record. You can then click in the field and edit, insert or delete data as necessary.

If you use [Tab] or [Shift]-[Tab] to move through fields, the contents of a field are selected when you move on to it.

◆ To replace the selected data within a field, simply key in the new text – this will replace the original data.

◆ To delete the data, press [**Delete**] when it is still selected.

◆ To add or delete data without removing the current contents, deselect the field contents first. Click into the field, or press [**F2**]. You can position the insertion point and edit as required.

To add a record:

1 Click the **New Record** tool ▸✳ on the Table Datasheet toolbar.

2 Enter your record details into the empty row.

To delete a record:

1 Place the insertion point within the record you wish to delete.

2 Click the **Delete Record** tool ✕ on the Table Datasheet toolbar.

6.7 Formatting in Datasheet view

If you don't like the formatting on your datasheet you can try something else. The Font, Datasheet, Row Height and Column Width options described below are applied to the whole table – you don't need to select anything first.

To set the font:

1 Choose **Font...** from the **Format** menu.

2 Select the font style, size and attributes required.

3 Click **OK**.

To set the Datasheet options:

1 Choose **Datasheet...** from the **Format** menu.

2 Specify the **Cell Effect, Background Color,** which **Gridlines** to show, the **Gridline Color** and the **Border and Line styles.**

3 Click **OK**.

To set the row height:

1 Choose **Row Height...** from the **Format** menu.

2 Specify a row height, or select the **Standard Height** checkbox.

3 Click **OK**.

To set the column width:

1 Place the insertion point anywhere within the column.

2 Choose **Column Width...** from the **Format** menu.

3 Specify the width or select **Standard Width** and click **OK**.

Or

♦ Let Access work out the best size by choosing *Best Fit*.

6.8 Changing the table structure

To edit the table structure you must take your table into Design view. You can do this from the Database window if you select the table you need to edit on the Tables tab, and click Design.

If you are in Datasheet view, you can click the View tool to go into Design view.

♦ To move back into Datasheet view afterwards, click the View tool on the Table Design toolbar.

To add a new field at the end of the table:

♦ Scroll down until you reach the empty row under the existing fields. Enter the field name, data type and properties.

To add a new field between two existing fields:

1 Place the insertion point in the upper pane anywhere within the field that will be below your new field.

2 Click the **Insert Rows** tool – a new row is inserted above the one the insertion point is in.

3 Enter the field name, data type, etc. as required.

To delete a field:

1 Place the insertion point in the upper pane within the field.

2 Click the **Delete Rows** tool ⬛.

3 Respond to the prompt – choose **Yes** to delete the field, **No** if you've changed your mind.

Be careful when you delete fields – any data held within that field in your records will be lost.

To change the field properties:

1 Place the insertion point within the field in the upper pane.

2 Press **[F6]** to move to the lower pane.

3 Edit the properties as required.

4 Press **[F6]** to return to the upper pane.

When changing a field size, watch that you don't lose data. If you reduce the size, any record that has data in that field in excess of the new size will have the extra characters lopped off!

To change the field that has Primary Key status:

1 Place the insertion point within the field in the upper pane that you want to take Primary Key status.

2 Click the **Primary Key** tool.

To remove Primary Key status, and not give it to any other field:

1 Place the insertion point within the field in the upper pane that currently has Primary Key status.

2 Click the **Primary Key** tool.

To rename a field:

◆ Edit the name in the first column in the upper pane.

To move a field:

1 Click in the row selector bar to the left of the field.

2 Drag and drop the field into its new position – a thick dark horizontal line indicates where the field will move to.

To keep the fields in their new position you must save the design before you close your table.

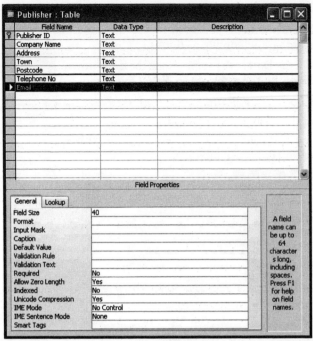

When you close your table, you will be asked if you wish to save the layout changes. Respond Yes (to save) or No (to close without saving) or Cancel (to return to the table to do more work).

6.9 AutoForm

As an alternative to entering data into a table in Datasheet view, you could use Form view.

In Datasheet view, each record is displayed in a row, each field in a column. As many fields and records are displayed in the table window as will fit.

In Form view, the fields are arranged attractively on the screen (you can design forms to resemble paper forms you actually use) and one record is displayed at a time. Form view is often considered more 'user friendly' than Datasheet view.

Access has a useful tool that builds a simple form automatically – AutoForm. Try it out by creating forms for your *Books* table and *Publisher* table.

To create an AutoForm for a table:

1 Select the table you wish to use from the Tables list in the Database window e.g. *Books*.

2 On the Database toolbar, click the drop-down arrow to the right of the **New Object** tool.

3 Choose **AutoForm**.

The table you selected is displayed using a simple form layout (*Books* table), or form with a subform (*Publisher* table).

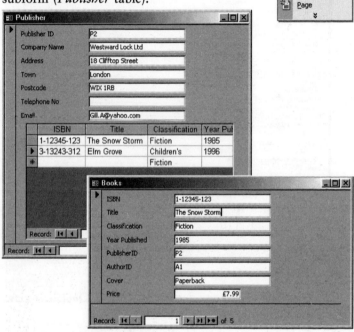

You can move around in Form view in the same way as you did in Datasheet view:

♦ Press **[Tab]** or **[Shift]-[Tab]** to move from field to field, or click in the field you want input or edit.

♦ Use the navigation buttons to move from record to record, or to the first or last record in the table.

♦ To go to a specific record number, click into the record number field, type the number you wish to go to and press **[Enter]**.

- Click the **New Record** button to get a blank form.
- Use the scroll bars to move around a large form.

The data you enter or edit in your form in Form view will be stored in the table on which the form is based. Even if you opt not to save that form, the data will still be stored in the table.

Changing views

When working with a form, you have three views that you should be familiar with – Design, Datasheet and Form.

To change views:

1 Click the drop-down arrow to the right of the **View** tool.

2 Click on the view required.

6.10 Form Design

The actual *design* of a form can be viewed and adjusted in the Form Design window.

To take your form into Design view:

- Choose **Design View** from the View options.

The Form Design window will appear on your screen.

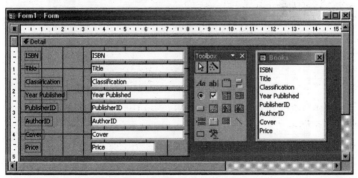

The Form is designed on a grid.

The Field List (displaying the field names from the table on which you are building the form) and the Toolbox (used to add labels, lines, etc. to your form) may also be displayed.

- Click the **Toolbox** tool  to toggle the display of the Toolbox.

- Click the **Field List** tool to toggle the Field List display.

Form areas

The main areas in a form:

- Detail area
- Form header and footer area
- Page header and footer area.

The detail area is present on every form. It is the part in which most of the detail from your table will be displayed.

The form header and footer areas appear above and below the detail area for each record in Form view. Form headers and footers are used for titles or instructions you wish to appear above and below each form.

To toggle the form header and footer on and off:

1 Open the **View** menu.

2 Choose **Form Header/Footer**.

The page header and footer areas appear at the top and bottom of each page, should you opt to print your form out.

To toggle the page header and footer on and off:

1 Open the **View** menu.

2 Choose **Page Header/Footer**.

If you enter any data into the Form or Page Header or Footer area, then opt *not* to display it, the data you entered will be lost.

The form above could be modified by adding a heading (in the Form Header area) containing the text 'Library Book Details'. The text 'Library Book Details' would be placed in a *label*.

Labels are used for instructions or headings – in fact any text that doesn't come from the underlying table.

Text

To add the text:

1 Display the form header and footer areas.

2 Click the **Label** tool in the Toolbox.

3 Move the pointer into the form header area (notice that the pointer now looks like this: +A).

4 Click in the form header area where you want your heading to go.

5 Key in your heading.

6 Click anywhere outside the label field.

♦ To resize the form header or footer area, drag its bottom edge (the pointer changes to a black double-headed arrow when you are in the correct place).

Objects

The objects (fields, labels, etc.) on your form can be moved, resized, formatted or deleted – so it's not critical that you get everything right first time.

Before you can edit an object in any way, you must click on it to select it. You will notice that a selected object has 'handles' around it – one in each corner and one halfway along each side.

- **To resize:** click and drag a handle in the direction required.

- **To move:** point to its edge (not over a handle) and drag – the pointer looks like a hand when you are in the correct place.

- **To delete a field:** select it and press [**Delete**].

- **To change the formatting:** use the tools on the Formatting (Form/Report) toolbar.

You could format the heading that you put on your *Books* form. If you increase the size of the font, you may need to increase the size of the label so that all of the text is displayed.

- To make a form wider, drag its right-most edge.

Pictures

To add a picture to your form:

1 Display and/or resize the area where you want the picture, e.g. form header area, or form footer area or detail area.

2 Select the **Image** tool 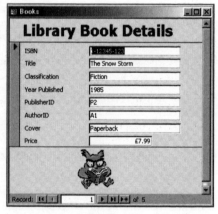 in the Toolbox.

3 Click in the area that you want the picture.

4 At the **Insert Picture** dialog box, locate and select the picture – double-click on it.

5 You will be returned to your form.

6 Resize/move your picture as necessary.

Experiment with the picture size mode to see the various effects.

1 Double-click on the picture to open the **Properties** dialog box.

2 Locate the **Size Mode** field (the third one on the **Format** tab or fourth on the **All** tab).

3 Select *Clip*, *Stretch* or *Zoom* as required.

4 Close the dialog box – click **Close**.

If you do not like the effect, repeat steps 1–4 and try another.

Background colour

To change the background colour of your form:

1 Select the area to format – detail, header, footer, etc.

2 Click the drop-down arrow by the **Fill/Back color** tool.

3 Choose a colour.

♦ Choose **Form View** from the **View** options to display your results.

Saving your form

To save your form, click the **Save** tool on the Form Design toolbar. At the **Save As** dialog box, accept the default form name, or edit it, and click **OK**.

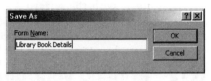

If you close your form without first saving it, Access will ask you if you want to save the form.

♦ **Yes** will take you to the **Save As** dialog box.

♦ **No** will close the form without saving it.

♦ **Cancel** will return you to Form view.

If you save your form, it will be listed under Forms in the Database window. To open the form again from here, either double-click on its name or select the name and click **Open**.

6.11   Form Wizard

You can also create a form using the Form Wizard. Use this where the fields are taken from more than one table, and when you want to use a preset colour scheme/design.

1 Select **Forms** in the Objects bar.

2 Double-click Create form by using wizard.

3 Select the table or query you wish to use a field from.

4 Select the field. Click to add it to the *selected fields* list.

5 Repeat steps 3–4 until all fields have been added, then click **Next**.

6 If you have selected fields from more than one table or query, you will be asked how you want to view the form – explore the options and select the one required.

7 Choose a layout and click **Next**.

8 Select a style, and then click **Next**.

9 Amend the suggested Form name(s) if you wish.

10 Select *Open the form to view or edit information*.

11 Click **Finish**.

♦ Experiment with the wizard – you can create some useful forms very easily this way. If you wish to tweak the form, take it into Design view and work on it there.

6.12 Printing your tables

You can print the contents of your tables from Datasheet view or from the Database window (simply select the table you want to print before you click the Print tool). See section 3.4 for more on Preview and Print.

Margins and orientation

If you need to change the margins or the orientation of your table before you print, you must go into the Page Setup options.

To view the Page Setup options:

1 Open your table in Datasheet view.

2 Select **Page Setup...** from the **File** menu.

♦ On the **Margins** tab of the dialog box, you can change the top, bottom, left or right margins. You can also specify whether or not to print the field name at the top of each field – use the *Print headings* option.

♦ On the **Page** tab, you can change the orientation (portrait or landscape), the paper size and source details, and the printer details.

6.13 Sort

You can easily sort the records in a table into ascending or descending order.

1 Open the table you are going to sort.

2 Place the insertion point anywhere within the field you want to sort the records on.

3 Click the **Sort Ascending** ![] or **Sort Descending** ![] tool.

When you close a table that you have sorted, you will be asked if you want to save the changes. To save the records in the new, sorted order, choose **Yes**, otherwise choose **No**.

Multi-level sort

If you want to sort your table on several fields, you must set up your sort requirements in the Filter dialog box. You could sort your *Books* table into ascending order on Classification, then by Title. Open your *Books* table to try this out.

1 Open the **Records** menu, point to **Filter** and select **Advanced Filter/Sort...**

♦ In the upper half of the **Filter** dialog box the field list of the current table is displayed. Scroll through the list until you see the field you want to use for your main sort.

2 Double-click on the field name required – it will appear in the first row, first column of the query grid.

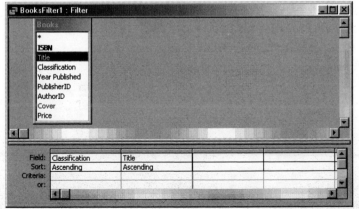

3 Select the options in the **Sort** row below the field name.

4 Return to the upper pane and double-click on the field for your second-level sort.

5 Click the **Apply Filter** tool 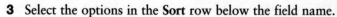 on the Filter/Sort toolbar to display your records in the new order.

You can save the options you have set up as a Query. You must return to the **Filter** dialog box to do this (use **Records > Filter > Advanced Filter/Sort...**).

1 Click the **Save As Query** tool 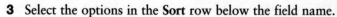 on the Filter/Sort toolbar.

2 Give your query a suitable name.

3 Click **OK**.

It will be listed under Queries in the Database window.

6.14 Find

To locate a record in your table, you can use the navigation buttons, or go to a record by specifying its number in the number field within the navigation buttons and pressing [Enter]. You can also locate records using Find.

1 In Datasheet view, place the insertion point within the field that contains the text you want to find.

2 Click the **Find** tool 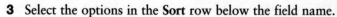 on the Table Datasheet toolbar.

3 Type what you are looking for in the **Find What:** field.

4 Edit the other fields as necessary.

5 Click **Find Next** to find the first matching record.

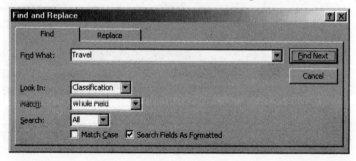

6 If it is not the record you want, click **Find Next** until you reach the correct record.

7 Close the dialog box once you have found your record.

If Access can't find what you are looking for, a dialog box will appear telling you that the search string wasn't found. If this happens, check your entry in the Find What: field carefully – you may have typed it in incorrectly.

6.15 Filter

If you want to display a specific group of records, this can be done by filtering them. You can filter 'By Selection' or 'By Form'.

Filter By Selection

1 Open the table in Datasheet view if necessary.

2 Position the insertion point in the field of a record that has the criterion you are looking for.

3 Click the **Filter By Selection** tool .

A subset of the records within your table will be displayed.

♦ You can filter your filtered list using the same technique – narrowing down your list of records as you go.

♦ To display all your records, click the **Remove Filter** tool ▼ .

Filter By Form

When you Filter By Form, you can specify multiple criteria (unlike Filter By Selection where you narrow down your search one criterion at a time). You can also use operators in your search.

Operators

To set a range of values, use these operators in your expressions:

<	Less than	>	Greater than
<=	Less than or equal to	>=	Greater than or equal to
=	Equal to	<>	Not equal to
Is Null	Empty field	Is Not Null	Field has an entry in it

You can also set a range with the keywords **Between...And...**

To filter by form:

1 Click the **Filter By Form** tool.

◆ You are presented with an empty record. As you move from field to field, notice you can display a list of options for each.

2 Select the filter criteria using the drop-down lists, and/or type in your criteria using the appropriate operators.

3 Click the **Apply Filter** tool ▽ – all records meeting the criteria specified will be displayed.

4 To display all your records again, click **Remove Filter** ▽.

As with a multi-level sort in section 6.13, you can save the options you have specified in the Filter by Form window as a Query.

1 Click the **Save As Query** tool on the **Filter/Sort** toolbar.

2 Give your query a suitable name.

3 Click **OK**.

It will be listed under Queries in the Database window.

6.16 Query Design

You can also sort your data, or specify select criteria, in Query Design view.

Using Query Design view:

1 Select **Queries** in the Objects bar.

2 Double-click Create query in Design view.

You will arrive at the Select Query dialog box. The Show Table window should be open, listing the tables in your database.

◆ If the Show Table window is not open, click the **Show Table** tool to display the table list.

3 Add the table(s) required to the **Select Query** dialog box – *Publisher* in this example.

4 Close the Show Table window.

You will notice some extra rows in the lower pane of the Select Query window.

♦ The **Table** row displays the name of the table from which a field is taken.

♦ The sort order is specified in the **Sort** row.

♦ The **Show** row indicates whether or not a selected field will be displayed in the result – a tick in the box means the field detail will be displayed. The default is to display the detail.

♦ The **Criteria** row(s) is where you tell Access the rules that you want to apply for selection.

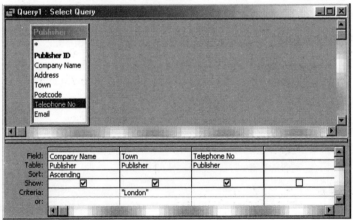

1 Select the fields you want, in the order you want them to appear – double-click on them in the field list.

2 Specify the sort order and/or criteria.

♦ In this example, we want publishers based in London, sorted into ascending order on Company name.

3 Run your query – click the **Run** tool ![Run] on the Query Design toolbar.

4 Save your query if you want to reuse it.

5 Close your query.

Specifying criteria

The criteria are specified through expressions that you key into
the criteria rows in the query grid. When entering expressions
there are a couple of rules you should keep in mind.

* When you enter criteria in different cells in the same criteria
  row, Access uses the **And** operator. It looks for **all** the condi-
  tions being met before returning the record details.

* If you enter criteria in different cells in different criteria rows,
  Access uses the **Or** operator.

Querying multiple tables

There may be times when you need to collect data from several
tables, and sort or filter that data. When working across several
tables, you must set up a query in the Query Design window. In
this example a query is used to produce a list of authors' names,
the titles of their books, and the name of the publisher.

1 Work through steps 1–4 in Query Design above – opt to show
all three tables at the **Show Table** dialog box.

2 Specify the criteria and sort order.

3 Save the query.

4 Run it.

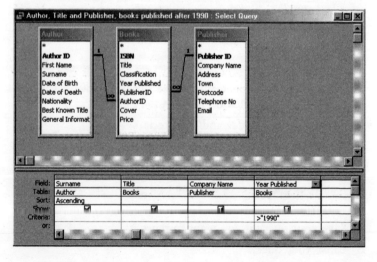

The main purpose (and strength) of a database is to enable you to store your data (maybe tens of thousands of records in a real business situation) and quickly extract or sort that data as required. Experiment with the query and sorting facilities until you get the hang of them. See section 6.15 for details of the operators you can use.

Try these ones:

Books table

- Extract details of all Fiction written since 1985.
- Display details of Title, Classification and Price, sorted into Price order.
- Display a list of all book details *except* those classified as Travel (<>Travel).

Publisher table

- Extract Name, Town and Telephone No., displaying details of the publishers that you *do not* have a telephone number for (Telephone No = "Is Null").
- Display publisher Name, Town and Email, in Town order.

Multiple table queries

- Display the publisher name, book title and price for all the London publishers.
- Extract a list showing publisher name, author name, and book title for all books priced between £8 and £12.

Wildcards

When querying your tables you can use *wildcards* to represent either a string of characters or a single character.

- * can be used to represent a string
- ? can be used to represent a single character

Step* in the Surname field would return *Stephen, Stephenson, Steptoe*, etc.

S?t in any field would return *sat, set, sit*.

6.17 AutoReport

Reports are used to display the data in your tables and queries in a layout that is usually easier to interpret than the datasheet.

You can quickly design a simple report (in much the same way as you generate an AutoForm) from any table or query using the AutoReport object. It will be a simple, single column report, listing all the fields in each record of the table or query.

To create an AutoReport from a table or query:

1 Display the **New Object** list.

2 Select **AutoReport**.

♦ A simple report will be created using the data in the table or query you have open.

3 When you close your report you will be asked if you want to save it. If you save it, it will be listed under Reports in the Database window.

You do not need to open a table or query to create an AutoReport from it – you can do so from the Database window.

To generate an AutoReport from the Database window:

1 Select the table or query you want to base your report on.

2 Choose **AutoReport** from the **New Object** list.

Reports are displayed in Print Preview – so you can see what your page would look like if you were to print it out.

You can use the navigation buttons at the bottom of the Print Preview window to move through the pages in your report.

♦ Click the **View** tool on the Print Preview toolbar to take your report through into Design view.

6.18 Report Wizard

You can also create a report using the Report Wizard, in a similar way to creating a form using Form Wizard (see section 6.11). This option is *very* useful if you wish to group the information in your report in any way, e.g. group books by classification. You can also perform simple summary calculations over the group, and over the whole report using the summary options.

In this example, we will display our books in a report, grouped by Classification. The books will be sorted into ascending order on Title. We will perform a summary calculation on the Price field, to display the average price in each classification.

1 Select **Reports** in the Objects bar.

2 Double-click 🗐 `Create report by using wizard`.

3 Select the Books table, and add all the fields to the *Selected Fields* list and click **Next**.

4 Specify the grouping – *Classification* in this example – and click **Next**.

5 Set the sort order – *Title*.

6 Click **Summary Options...**

7 Select **Avg** in the **Summary Options** dialog box, and select **Detail and Summary** in the **Show** options, click **OK**.

8 Click **Next**.

9 Select a layout and specify the orientation for the page (if you have a lot of fields to display use landscape).

10 Select the checkbox **Adjust the field width so all fields fit on a page** and click **Next**.

11 Choose a **Style** and click **Next**.

12 Edit the name, select **Preview the Report** and click **Finish**.

Book

Classification	Title	ISBN	Year Publish	PublisherID	AuthorID	Cover	Price
Children's	Elm Grove	3-13243-31	1996	P2	A4	Paperback	£6.99
Summary for 'Classification' = Children's (1 detail record)							
Avg							£6.99
Fiction	The Lying Stone	5-11111-22	1954	P4	A3	Hardback	£16.99
	The Snow Storm	1-12345-12	1985	P2	A1	Paperback	£7.99
Summary for 'Classification' = Fiction (2 detail records)							
Avg							£12.49
Travel	Africa Trekker	4-53423-22	1994	P1	A2	Paperback	£6.99
	Indian Highlights	2-54321-32	1997	P3	A2	Paperback	£9.99
Summary for 'Classification' = Travel (2 detail records)							
Avg							£8.49

17 June 2003   *Page 1 of 1*

You can take the report into Design view and edit it in a similar way to editing a form in Design view.

◆ Experiment with the wizard – you can design some attractive and useful reports with it quite easily.

6.19 Report Design

The Design view of a report looks very similar to the Design view of a form. You should experiment with it so that you can control the look of your reports even more.

The main areas in a report:

◆ Detail area

◆ Page header and footer area

◆ Report header and footer area.

The commands to switch the page and/or report header and footer areas on and off are in the View menu.

◆ The page header and footer area are displayed by default in an AutoReport design.

The field list, containing the field names from the table or query on which the report is based, is displayed – you can toggle the display of this by clicking the **Field List** tool ▣.

Page header and footer

Page headers are often used for column headings, or the report title, page footers are usually used for page numbering.

You can add a page header using the **Label** tool. You used this in Form design to add headings, instructions and other text to your form. The same techniques are used in Report design.

In the page footer area of a report, the page number is usually shown, placed in a text box. If you have created a report and it doesn't have page numbers, you can add them in Design view.

1 If necessary, scroll down through your form until you see the page footer area.

2 Click the **Text Box** tool then click and drag in the page footer area to indicate the position of the text box.

- A text box field consists of a description (the left part) and a detail area (the right part).

3 Edit the text in the description part, or delete the description – select it and press **[Delete]**.

To put a page number in the detail part of the text box:

1 Click on the box to select it.

2 Type '=[Page]' in the field.

Grouping

If you didn't use the wizard to specify grouping for a report, you can group (or ungroup) the records from Design view.

Grouping is specified in the Sorting and Grouping dialog box.

1 Click the **Sorting and Grouping** tool [≡ on the Report Design toolbar.

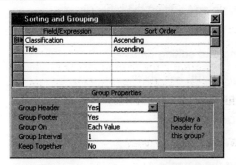

2 Set the **Field/Expression** area – select the field you want to group on from the drop-down list, e.g. *Classification*.

3 Set the **Sort Order**.

4 In the **Group Properties** pane, set the **Group Header** property to **Yes** (to put the classification at the top of each group).

5 Specify any other fields you want sorted in the dialog box.

6 Close the dialog box to return to your design grid.

7 Add fields, text, etc. as required into the group header and/ or footer.

Finishing touches

Using the Toolbox and the Formatting toolbar, you can add the finishing touches to the objects in your report (or form) by adding lines, borders, colour and special effects. There are instructions to help get you started in Chapter 3.

Summary

This chapter has discussed setting up and manipulating a database using Microsoft Access. Topics covered included:

* Planning and designing a database
* Database jargon and Access objects
* Primary Key
* Data types and properties
* Setting up and editing the table design
* Relationships
* Entering and editing data
* Formatting the datasheet
* AutoForm
* Form Design view
* Form Wizard
* Printing the datasheet
* Sorting data on single and multiple fields
* Using Find to locate records
* Extracting records using the Filter option
* Setting up and running a simple Query
* AutoReport
* Report Wizard
* Report Design view.

07

presentations

In this chapter you will learn

- about PowerPoint and presentations
- how to create slides and handouts
- how to add tables and charts
- how to prepare and deliver a presentation

7.1 Introduction to PowerPoint

You can use PowerPoint to produce:

Slides – the individual pages of a presentation. They may contain text, graphs, clip art, tables, drawings, animation, video clips, visuals from other applications – and more!! PowerPoint will allow you to present your slides via a slide show on your computer, 35mm slides or overhead projector transparencies.

Notes Pages – to accompany your slides. Each notes page has a small image of the slide plus any typed notes. You can print the pages and use them to prompt you during a presentation.

Handouts – smaller versions of your slides, printed 2, 3, 6 or 9 slides to a page. They provide backup material for your audience and can be customized with a company name or logo.

Outline – a useful overview of your presentation's structure, this has the slide titles and main text items, but no art work.

Getting started

When you start PowerPoint a new blank presentation is created automatically, with a blank Title slide. The Getting Started task pane is displayed (unless the option has been turned off).

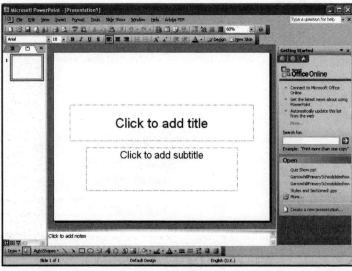

The boxes with dotted outlines that appear when you create a new slide are called placeholders.

The PowerPoint window is very similar to other Office application windows. The Standard and Formatting toolbars usually appear along the top of the window. The Drawing toolbar is usually along the bottom of the window.

If you are ready to start work on a new presentation, close the task pane so that there is more room for your work.

- You can keep the task pane open if you prefer, it's up to you.

PowerPoint objects

The text and graphics that you can place on a slide in PowerPoint are called objects. An object may be:

- Text
- Drawings
- Graphs
- Tables
- WordArt
- Clip art
- Movies
- Sounds
- Organization charts or other diagrams

Different slide layouts have different placeholders – these will contain the slide title, text and any other objects on your slide.

1 Follow the prompts on the slide – enter the title and subtitle (if required) for your presentation.

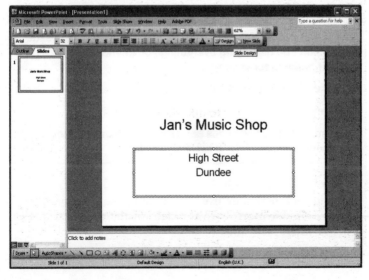

2   Click the **New Slide** tool 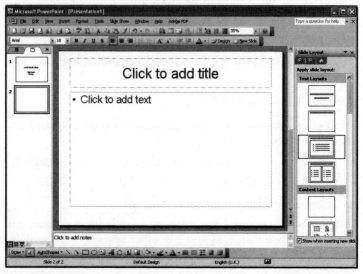.

3   Select a slide layout from the Slide Layout task pane (a single bulleted list layout is the default).

4   Enter your text – follow the prompts.

5   Repeat steps 2–4 until all slides have been added.

Remember the 666 rule!

It is good to try to be concise on your text slides – the slide shouldn't be displaying everything you intend to say – just a brief heading for your topic.

No more than 6 words to a bullet point.

No more than 6 bullet points to a slide.

No more than 6 text slides before you break the presentation up with a graphic e.g. a table or chart.

Things to note/experiment with

•   To insert a new slide from the Slide Layout task pane, click the drop-down arrow to the right of the slide layout, then click **Insert New Slide**.

•   You can resize the task pane by dragging its left border.

- Use the arrows at the top left of the task pane to move between the New Presentation and the Slide Layout task panes.

- Scroll through the list of layouts to display the various types of layout, e.g. Text, Content, Text and Content, and Other.

- Some of the slide layouts in the Slide Layout task pane have graphic, table, organization chart and clip art objects set up on them. We will look at these later.

7.2 Creating a new presentation

When the New Presentation task pane is displayed, you can create a new presentation in a number of ways.

- **Blank Presentation** creates a new blank presentation and displays the Slide Layout task pane (see above).

- **From Design Template** creates a new presentation and displays the Slide Design task pane so you can choose a template on which to base your presentation (the template will determine the design elements of you presentation, including font and colour scheme).

- **From AutoContent Wizard** creates a new presentation and starts a wizard to step you through the process of setting up your title slide, outline of presentation and colour scheme.

- **From Existing Presentation** creates a new file by copying an existing one so you can edit it as required.

Design Template

To create a presentation using the Design Template option:

1 Click **From Design Template** on the New Presentation task pane.

2 Select a template from those listed (or click **Browse...** and locate the template to use).

3 Complete the Title Slide, e.g. Click to add title, click to add subtitle.

4 Click the ⌐New Slide tool on the Formatting toolbar.

5 Select the layout required for your next slide.

6 Follow the instructions on the slide to complete it.

7 Repeat steps 4–6 until all slides have been added.

If you don't like the look of your selected template, change it from the Slide Design task pane. To display this:

• Click the 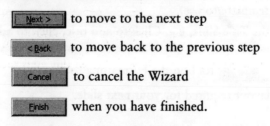 tool on the Formatting toolbar.

• Click the arrows at the top left of the task pane until the Slide Design task pane is displayed.

Or

• Double-click on the template name on the Status bar.

AutoContent Wizard

The AutoContent Wizard sets up several slides – the exact number depends on the choices you make as you work through the Wizard. If you need help setting up the structure of your presentation, or need some ideas on what to put on your slides, this option may be useful.

1 Click **From AutoContent Wizard** on the task pane.

2 Click Next > .

3 Pick the option that best describes the type of presentation you are going to give.

4 Select the presentation style – on-screen, Web, overheads or slides.

5 Enter the presentation title and any information that you want displayed in the slide footer area.

6 At the last screen, click Finish . PowerPoint will set up your presentation.

Working through the Wizard, click:

  Next > to move to the next step

  < Back to move back to the previous step

  Cancel to cancel the Wizard

  Finish when you have finished.

- Once a presentation has been created (using any of the above options) you can easily add or delete slides, change slide layouts or change the design template used.

You can create a new blank presentation by clicking the **New** tool on the Standard toolbar, or by pressing [**Ctrl**]-[**N**].

- If you have closed the New Presentation task pane, open the **File** menu and choose **New...** or open the **View** menu and choose **Task Pane** to display it again, if necessary.

7.3 View options

When working on a presentation, there are three view options to choose from:

- Normal view
- Slide Sorter view
- Slide Show

By default, PowerPoint displays all new presentations in Normal view.

Use the icons ▣▦▤ at the bottom left of the screen to change the view of your presentation. You can also change views using the View menu.

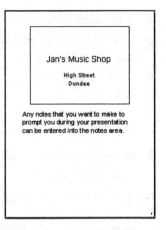

The View menu has an additional option called Notes Page view. This displays a miniature of your slide, with the notes area below it, showing how it will look when printed. You can also enter and edit notes in this view. If you wish to do this, use the Zoom tool on the Standard toolbar to zoom into about 75% so that you can read the text.

In Slide Sorter view, each slide is displayed in miniature – this view can be used for moving slides around and to help you prepare for the actual presentation. We will discuss this view later.

Slide Show view can be useful at any time to let you see how your slide will look in the final presentation. Press **[Esc]** from Slide Show view to return to your presentation file.

The view that you will use when setting up your presentation is Normal view. In Normal view, you have three panes displaying different parts of your presentation. The slide itself is in the top right (the Slide pane), notes are displayed in the bottom right (the Notes pane) and the outline and slide tabs are displayed down the left (Outline and Slides pane).

A task pane will often be displayed too.

Outline and Slides pane

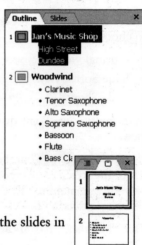

In Normal view the Outline and Slides pane is displayed on the left of the screen.

The Outline tab displays the text on each slide, with a slide icon to the left of each slide title. You can select a slide by clicking on this.

You can insert and delete text in the Outline tab just as you would on the Slide itself.

The Slides tab displays miniatures of the slides in your presentation.

Notes pane

As the presenter, you may wish to add some notes (that you can use during your presentation) to some of your slides.

Notes are added to the Notes pane, or in Notes Page view – see above.

To add notes to the Notes pane:

1 Click in the Notes pane.
2 Type in your notes.

Hide/Restore panes

◆ Click the **Close** button at the top right of the Outline and Slides pane to hide the pane.

Both the Outline and Slides pane and the Notes pane disappear.

◆ Click the Normal view icon or open the **View** menu and choose **Normal (Restore Panes)** to restore the pane.

To resize the panes: drag the pane border.

7.4 Working with slides

There are three ways that you can move through the slides in your presentation:

◆ Click on the slide that you wish to display on the Slides tab.

◆ Click the **Next Slide** or **Previous Slide** button at the bottom of the vertical scroll bar.

◆ Drag the elevator on the vertical scroll bar up and down.

Click on the slide icon

Drag the elevator

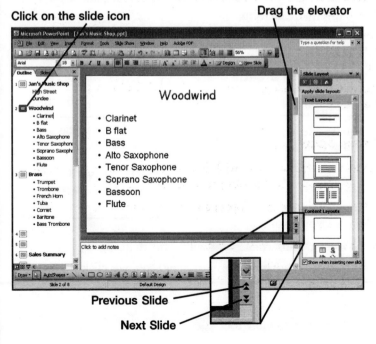

Previous Slide

Next Slide

Once you've created your presentation, the next step is to decide on the text that you want on your slides – the title, and the main points that you want to discuss during your presentation.

The main text on a slide will be in the title or bulleted list area.

You can determine the structure of the text on each slide (main points, sub-points, etc.), using up to 5 levels if necessary.

To edit text:

1 Locate the slide you want to edit.

2 Click to place the insertion point inside the text to be edited.

3 Insert or delete characters as required.

• If you want to change the text completely, select the old text (click and drag over it) and key in the replacement text.

To add new slides:

You can add new slides at any place in your presentation.

1 View the slide that you want above your new one.

2 Click the **New Slide** tool ⬚ New Slide on the Standard toolbar (not the **New** tool).

3 Select a layout.

Structuring a slide

The points you want to make on your slides will be structured – you will have main points (at the first bulleted level) and some of these points will have sub-points (at the second, third, fourth or fifth level). Initially, all points are at level 1. You can demote sub-items if necessary (and promote them again if you change your mind).

Slide Title
Level 1
Level 2
Level 3
Level 4
Level 5

1 Place the insertion point within the item.

2 On the Formatting (or Outlining) toolbar, click the **Demote** tool ⬚.

Or

• Click the **Promote** tool ⬚.

Moving bullet points

You can easily rearrange the points on your slide using cut and paste or drag and drop techniques, or click inside the item you wish to move and press [Shift]-[Alt]-[↑] to move an item up, [Shift]-[Alt]-[↓] to move an item down.

To move slides:

* Drag and drop the slide miniatures to move the slides in the Slides pane in Normal view or in Slide Sorter view.

To delete slides:

1 Select the slide miniature in the Slides pane in Normal view.

2 Press [Delete].

7.5 Formatting

Most of the formatting options, e.g. bold, alignment, and bullets work in the same way as in all other applications. Formatting options covered here are unique to PowerPoint.

To change a slide layout:

If you have chosen the wrong layout, it is easily changed.

1 View the slide whose layout you wish to change.

2 Display the Slide Layout task pane (use the arrow at the top of the task pane, or click the **Slide Layout** tool [⊞ Slide Layout...] on the Standard toolbar).

3 Select the layout required.

To increase/decrease paragraph spacing:

1 Select the paragraphs.

2 Click **Increase** [≣] or **Decrease** [≣] paragraph spacing to get your text evenly distributed on your slide.

* You'll find the tools on the **Formatting** toolbar under **Add or Remove buttons...** if they aren't already on the toolbar.

To change the design template:

The design template determines the colour, fonts, alignment of text, etc. of your presentation. You can change it at any time.

1 Double-click the template name field on the Status bar.

Or

♦ Click  Design to display the Design task pane.

2 Select the template you want to use.

Background styles

When you select a template, the slide background colour and shading is picked up from its options. You can easily change the colour and shading while still retaining the other design elements.

If your presentation were in sections, e.g. on individual departments, or regional figures, you could set a different background colour for each section of your presentation.

1 Choose **Background...** from the **Format** menu.

2 Choose a **Background fill** option.

Or

3 **Click More Colors...** and/or **Fill Effects...**, to display more options, and then select from the dialog boxes and click **OK**.

4 Click Apply to apply it to the selected slide or Apply to All to apply to all slides in the presentation.

♦ Click Preview to see the effect

or Cancel to return to the presentation without changing the background.

♦ **To select several adjacent slides:** click on the first one, then **[Shift]**-click on the last one that you wish to select.

♦ **To select non-adjacent slides:** click on the first one, and then hold down **[Ctrl]** while you click on each of the others.

And yet more options.....

Experiment with the other options in the **Format** menu. **Font, Bullets and Numbering, Alignment** and **Line Spacing** are very similar to those found in the other Office applications.

You can select several slides at once in Slide Sorter view then change the colours of them all in one operation.

7.6 Headers and footers

To add numbers, the date, time or any other text to your slides, notes or handouts use the Header and Footer command.

1 Open the **View** menu.

2 Choose **Header and Footer...**

3 Select the appropriate tab – **Slide** or **Notes and Handouts**.

4 Tick the items you want to appear, giving details as needed.

5 Click or [Apply to All].

7.7 Charts

Charts can be useful if you have figures to present and feel that a graphical representation would be more effective than the figures themselves.

There are three main ways to set up your chart:

Using a Chart placeholder:

• Double-click in the Chart placeholder to add a chart.

Using a Content placeholder:

• Click the **Insert Chart** tool in the placeholder.

From a slide with no placeholder set:

• Click the **Insert Chart** tool [icon] on the Standard toolbar.

Datasheet and toolbars

Regardless of how you decide to create your chart, Microsoft Graph opens and a chart window is displayed. This has its own Standard and Formatting toolbars, and you will notice a Chart menu appear on the Menu bar. The options in the other menus change to ones suitable for working on charts.

There is also a small Datasheet window (which can be moved or resized as necessary), where you can key in the data that you want to chart. When working in Microsoft Graph the Help menu will give you access to Help pages on the program.

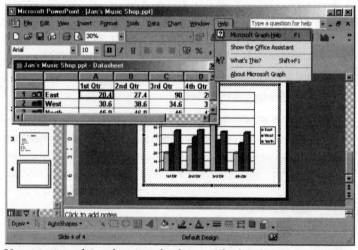

You must replace the sample data with the data you want to chart. If you do not need to replace all of it, delete the extra cell contents – select the column or row and press [Delete].

1 Select the cell into which you wish to enter your own data.

2 Key in the data.

3 Move to the next cell – use any of the methods shown below.

To move from cell to cell in the datasheet with the keyboard:

Arrow keys	one cell in direction of arrow
[Tab]	forward to the next cell
[Shift]-[Tab]	back to the previous cell
[Enter]	down to the next cell in a column

To move with the mouse:

◆ Point to the cell and click.

The cell you are in (your current cell) has a dark border.

View/hide datasheet

Once you have keyed in your data, you can hide the datasheet so you can see the chart clearly on your screen. If you hide your datasheet, you can view it again if you need to edit any data.

◆ Click the **View Datasheet** tool 🔲 on the Standard toolbar to view or hide the datasheet, as required.

7.8   Chart options

By Row and By Column

◆ The Category axis has labels taken from the column or row headings in your datasheet. Use **By Row** 🔲 and **By Column** 🔲 on the Standard toolbar to indicate whether your data series is in rows or columns. A graphic in the row or column heading of your datasheet indicates the selected option.

Chart type

The default chart type is a column chart. You can try out a variety of other chart types using the Chart Type tool on the Standard toolbar.

1 Click the drop-down arrow to display the chart types available.

2 Choose one.

◆ Open the **Chart** menu and choose **Chart Type...** You'll find lots of other options to choose from.

Hiding columns

If you don't want all your data to be displayed, you can hide rows or columns as required. This is done on the datasheet.

1 Display the datasheet if necessary.

2 Double-click on the heading of the column or row to hide.

♦ The data is dimmed, and is not displayed on your chart.

3 Double-click the heading again to unhide the column or row.

Colours and patterns

If you don't like the colour of a data series – the bars or lines representing one set of data – experiment with the options.

To change the colour of a data series:

1 With the chart selected, click on an item (e.g. bar or line) to select the series.

2 Click the **Fill Color** drop-down arrow on the Drawing toolbar.

3 Select a colour, or choose **Fill Effects** to display the dialog box and select from the gradients, textures and patterns.

To format any chart object:

1 Double-click on the object you wish to format.

2 Select the options from the **Format** dialog box.

3 Click **OK**.

Tour the options in the Format dialog boxes. They are full of features that can help you make the most of your chart!

Chart title and axis legends

To add a chart title or axis legend:

1 Open the **Chart** menu and choose **Options**.

2 Select the **Titles** tab.

3 Enter the titles as required and click **OK**.

To edit the title or legends:

1 Click the object once to select it.

2 Click again to place the insertion point within the text.

3 Edit as usual.

4 Click outside the object when finished.

To format the title or legend:

1 Click the object once to select it.

2 Use the tools on the **Formatting** toolbar.

Or

◆ Double-click on the object to open its **Format** dialog box.

To delete the title or legend:

1 Click the object once to select it.

2 Press [Delete].

> Use the Text Box and Arrow tools on the Drawing toolbar to add emphasis to your charts – see section 3.11.

Exiting Microsoft Graph

◆ When your chart is complete, click anywhere on the slide outside the chart placeholder to return to your presentation.

The whole chart becomes an object within your presentation, and can be moved, copied, deleted or resized as necessary.

◆ If you wish to edit your chart, simply double-click on it.

7.9 Organization charts

Organization charts give you another opportunity to make your point using a diagram rather than words. There are three main ways to set up your organization chart:

From a slide with the Diagram or Organization Chart placeholder:

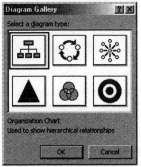

1 Double-click within the placeholder on your slide.

2 Select **Organization Chart** from the **Diagram Gallery** dialog box.

3 Click **OK**.

From a slide with a Contents placeholder:

1 Click the **Insert Diagram or Organization Chart** tool within the placeholder.

2 Select **Organization Chart** from the **Diagram Gallery** dialog box and click **OK**.

From a slide with no placeholder:

1 Click the **Insert Diagram or Organization Chart** tool 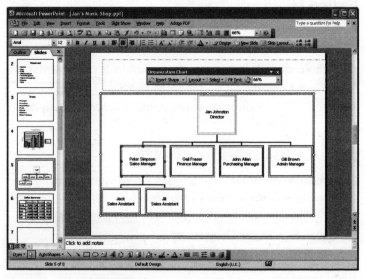 on the Drawing toolbar.

2 Select **Organization Chart** from the **Diagram Gallery** dialog box and click **OK**.

An organization chart object will be displayed on your slide.

Work out the structure you wish to display before you start. Don't try to display one that is too large — the finished slide should be clear and easy to understand.

Organization charts can be very complicated structures but they have only simple elements. The small set of tools in the Organization Chart toolbar is all that you need.

Text and boxes

To enter text into a box:

1 Click in the box you wish to edit.

2 Key in your data and press **[Enter]** or the arrow keys to move to the next row.

3 Click on the next box to be completed, or anywhere outside the box, when you are finished.

To add a box:

1 Click on the box to which the new box is related.

2 Click the **Insert Shape** on the Organization Chart toolbar.

3 Select the box type required.

To delete a box:

1 Click on the edge of the box to select it.

2 Press [Delete].

Layout

The default layout for an organization chart is the Standard one. You can easily change the layout for all or part of a chart.

To change the layout:

1 Select a 'manager' box – one that has subordinates.

2 Click the **Layout** button on the Organization Chart toolbar.

3 Select the layout option required.

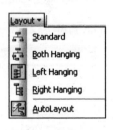

To select a set of boxes:

1 Select one of the boxes required.

2 Click the **Select** button on the Organization Chart toolbar.

3 Choose the group of boxes from the options available.

Autoformat

To quickly format the whole of your chart effectively:

1 Click the **Autoformat** tool on the Organization Chart toolbar.

2 Select an Autoformat.

3 Click **Apply**.

• Click outside the Organization Chart placeholder when you have finished.

Experiment with the other drawings that you can create from the Diagram Gallery dialog box.

7.10 Tables

If you have created tables using Word, you'll find it very easy to create them on your slides. The options for creating a table are similar to those for creating a graph or organization chart.

1 Select a slide layout with a **Table or Content** placeholder.

2 Click the **Insert Table** tool.

3 Specify the number of rows and columns and click **OK**.

On a slide without a Table or Content placeholder:

1 Click the **Insert Table** tool.

2 Drag over the grid to indicate the number of rows and columns required.

The Tables and Borders toolbar appears when a table is selected.

♦ If it doesn't appear, click the **Tables and Borders** tool 🔲.

When working in a table:

♦ Press [Tab] to move to the next cell, [Shift]-[Tab] to go to the previous cell or the arrow keys to move between them.

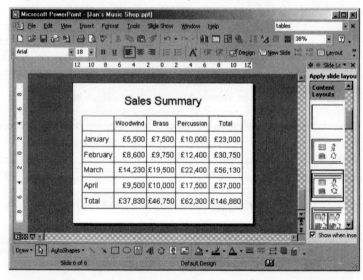

Sales Summary

	Woodwind	Brass	Percussion	Total
January	£5,500	£7,500	£10,000	£23,000
February	£8,600	£9,750	£12,400	£30,750
March	£14,230	£19,500	£22,400	£56,130
April	£9,500	£10,000	£17,500	£37,000
Total	£37,830	£46,750	£62,300	£146,880

Or using the mouse:

- Click in the cell you wish to work on.

- Click outside the table when you've finished.

- Click on your table again if you wish to edit it.

7.11   The Clip Gallery

PowerPoint comes with hundreds of clip art pictures that can be added to your slides. You'll find many more on the Internet.

To insert clip art into a slide:

1   Click the **Insert Clip Art** tool on the Drawing toolbar.

2   Enter your search keywords, e.g. food, music, animal.

3   Click on the picture required.

4   Move/resize the clip art as necessary.

To insert onto a slide with a Content or Clip Art placeholder:

- Click the **Insert Clip Art** tool in the **Content** placeholder, or double-click the **Clip Art** placeholder, then continue as above.

See section 3.12 for more on inserting clip art.

7.12   Masters

Masters are the templates on which slides, handouts and notes pages as based. They contain information on fonts, placeholder sizes and positions, design and colour schemes. They are used to set global formatting, or to add or remove a logo, picture or anything that will affect all the slides in the presentation.

Masters are added to a presentation when you apply a Design template. Most templates have a Slide Master and a Title Master (which may only be used for the Title slide). These are displayed as miniatures in the Slide pane when you view a master.

Slide Master

The Slide Master holds the formatted placeholders for the slide title and text. Any slides where you have made changes to the text formatting, etc. at slide level will be treated as exceptions and will retain the custom formatting you applied to them.

Any objects you want to appear on every slide (like your company name or logo) should be added to the Slide Master.

1 Choose **Master** from the **View** menu.

2 Select **Slide Master**.

3 Amend the Slide Master as required (using the same techniques that you use on ordinary slides).

4 Click **Close Slide Master**.

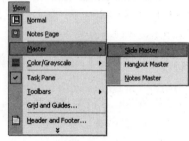

Or

Choose an alternative view to leave your Slide Master.

• Hold down **[Shift]** and click the Slide View 🔲 button, to go to the Slide Master, or to the Title Master if you are on the Title slide at the time.

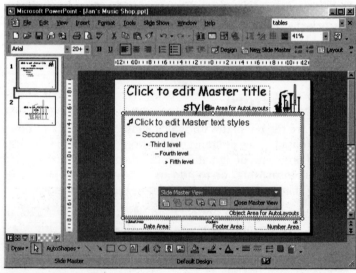

If you have no Title Master in your presentation you can easily add one (the Blank Presentation option does not have one).

1 View the Slide Master.

2 Click the **Insert New Title Master** tool 🔲 on the Slide Master View toolbar.

The placeholders

The object areas for AutoLayouts, Date Area, Footer Area or Number Area placeholders are all optional. They can be deleted – or put back again if you decide you want them after all.

To delete a placeholder:

• Select the placeholder and press [Delete].

To restore a placeholder:

1 Click the **Master Layout** tool.

2 Select the placeholders required.

3 Click OK.

7.13 Slide shows

The whole point of setting up a presentation is so that you can eventually deliver it to your audience. Once you've got your slides organized, there are a number of tools you can use to help you finalize your preparations.

Slide Sorter view

There are several useful features worth exploring in Slide Sorter view, including: hiding slides, setting up transitions, animating text on slides and rehearsing timings.

• Click the **Slide Sorter View tool** .

Slide Sorter toolbar

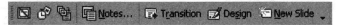

Hide Slide

This can prove useful if you're not sure if you really need a particular slide for your presentation. You can include the slide (in case it's needed), but hide it. The hidden slide will be bypassed during your slide show, unless you decide you need to use it.

1 Select the slide you want to hide.

2 Click the **Hide Slide** tool .

- The slide number is crossed out under the slide.

- If you want to show the hidden slide during a presentation press [H] at the slide preceding the hidden one.

- To remove the hidden status from a slide, select it and click the **Hide Slide** tool again.

Rehearse timings

It is a very good idea to practise your presentation before you end up in front of your audience. As well as practising what you intend to say (probably with the aid of notes you have made on the Notes page), you can rehearse the timings for each slide.

1 Click the **Rehearse Timings** tool 🕑 to go into your slide show for a practice run.

2 Go over what you intend to say while the slide is displayed.

3 Click to move to the next slide when ready.

4 Repeat steps 2 and 3 until you reach the end of your presentation.

A dialog box displays the total time of your presentation and asks if you want to use the timings in a slide show. Choose **Yes**, if you want each slide to advance after the allocated time.

> **Microsoft PowerPoint** ✕
>
> ℹ️ The total time for the slide show was 0:04:30. Do you want to keep the new slide timings to use when you view the slide show?
>
> [Yes] [No]

The slide timings will be displayed in Slide Sorter view.

- You can rehearse your timings as often as is necessary, until you've got the pace right to get your message across.

Summary Slide

You can get PowerPoint to automatically produce a Summary Slide for your presentation. The Summary Slide is placed in front of the other slides and lists the titles of the selected slides.

1 Select the slides from which to produce a Summary Slide.

2 Click the **Summary Slide** tool 🗐 on the Slide Sorter toolbar.

- PowerPoint will generate as many Summary Slides as is necessary to list the title detail from all the slides you select.

Notes

You can also add notes to your slides from Slide Sorter view.

1 Click the **Notes** tool 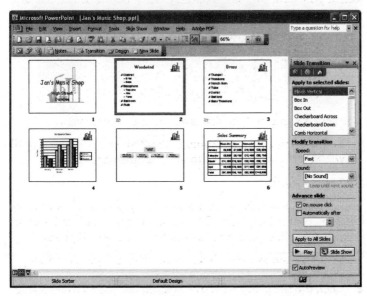 to open the **Notes** dialog box.
2 Select the slide that you wish to add or edit notes for.
3 Enter or edit the notes as required.
4 Repeat steps 2–3 for each slide as required.
5 Close the dialog box when you've finished.

Transitions

A transition is an effect used when a slide appears in a show. The default is to have no transitions, but are some interesting options that you might find effective in your presentation.

1 Select the slide(s) that you wish to give a transition effect.
2 Click the **Slide Transition** tool.
- The Slide Transition task pane is displayed.

3 Select the effect required from the list (it will preview if AutoPreview is selected at the bottom of the task pane).

4 Set the **Speed** to *Fast*. Focus your audience on your slides, not the transition method!

5 Select a **Sound** if you wish.

6 Choose an **Advance slide** option.

♦ *Apply to All* applies the effect to all slides in the presentation, not just the selected one(s).

♦ *Play* previews the effect on the selected slide.

♦ *Slide Show* displays the slide and effect in Slide Show view.

If a transition is set, a transition icon appears below the slide in Slide Sorter view. Click on it to see the effect.

Animation

If you have several points in the body text of your slide, you could try building the slide up, rather than presenting the whole list at once. Experiment with the Animation options and effects until you find the ones you prefer. You can have a lot of fun with the options – but avoid having a different effect on each slide!

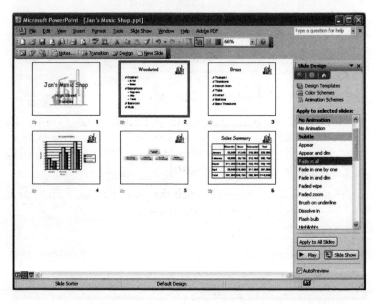

To set an animation effect:

1 Click the **Design** tool [≥ Design] to display the Design task pane.

2 Select **Animation Schemes** on the Slide Design task pane.

3 Select the slide(s) you wish to animate.

4 Pick an effect from the list.

5 Click **Apply to All Slides** if you want all slides affected.

6 Close the task pane when you have made your settings.

7.14   Slide Show

You can run your slide show at any time to check how your presentation is progressing. Each slide fills the whole of your screen. After the last, you are returned to the view you were in when you clicked the Slide Show tool.

1 Select the slide you want to start from, usually the first.

2 Click the **Slide Show** icon [🖳] to the left of the horizontal scroll bar.

3 Click, or press **[Page Down]** or **[Enter]** to go to the next slide.

♦ Press **[Page Up]** to go back to the previous slide if necessary.

♦ You can exit your slide show at any time by pressing **[Esc]**.

Working within your slide show

When presenting your slide show, you might want to leave the normal sequence, go directly to a slide, or draw on a slide to focus attention. These, and other features, can be accessed using the pop-up menu or the keyboard.

1 Right-click anywhere, or click the pop-up menu icon [▦] at the bottom left corner of the screen.

To go directly to a slide:

2 Select **Go to Slide**.

3 Choose the slide you want to go to.

♦ Explore the options on the pop-up menu.

To draw on your screen:

1 Press [Ctrl]-[P] to change the pointer to a pen.

2 Click and drag to draw.

3 Press [Ctrl]-[A] to change the pointer back to an arrow.

To erase your drawing:

♦ Press [E].

To get more help on the options available to you while running Slide Show, press [F1]. The **Slide Show Help** dialog box lists other options you might want to experiment with.

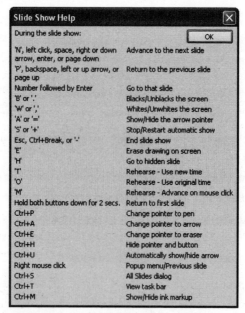

Slide Show Help	
During the slide show:	OK
'N', left click, space, right or down arrow, enter, or page down	Advance to the next slide
'P', backspace, left or up arrow, or page up	Return to the previous slide
Number followed by Enter	Go to that slide
'B' or '.'	Blacks/Unblacks the screen
'W' or ','	Whites/Unwhites the screen
'A' or '='	Show/Hide the arrow pointer
'S' or '+'	Stop/Restart automatic show
Esc, Ctrl+Break, or '-'	End slide show
'E'	Erase drawing on screen
'H'	Go to hidden slide
'T'	Rehearse - Use new time
'O'	Rehearse - Use original time
'M'	Rehearse - Advance on mouse click
Hold both buttons down for 2 secs.	Return to first slide
Ctrl+P	Change pointer to pen
Ctrl+A	Change pointer to arrow
Ctrl+E	Change pointer to eraser
Ctrl+H	Hide pointer and button
Ctrl+U	Automatically show/hide arrow
Right mouse click	Popup menu/Previous slide
Ctrl+S	All Slides dialog
Ctrl+T	View task bar
Ctrl+M	Show/Hide ink markup

7.15 Printing presentations

You can print your whole presentation – the slides, speaker's notes pages, audience handouts and the presentation outline.

The first stage to printing is to set up the format.

1 Choose **Page Setup** from the **File** menu.

2 Select the size from the **Slides sized for** field.

3 Specify the orientation for the **Slides**.

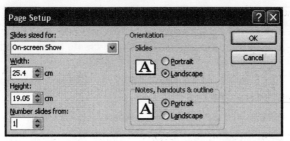

4 Specify the orientation for the **Notes, handouts & outline.**

5 Click **OK.**

Printing

With the Page Setup details specified to give the output required, you can go ahead and print. If you click the Print icon, one copy of each slide is printed. To print anything else you must access the Print dialog box and specify what you want to print.

1 Open the **File** menu and choose **Print.**

2 Specify the **Print range** – *All, Current Slide, Selection* or *Slides*.

3 Select the option required in the **Print what:** list.

Slides – prints your slides one slide per page.

Handouts – prints miniatures of the slides, 2, 3, 6 or 9 to the page. Printing your handouts with 3 slides to the page is particularly useful as there is room for your audience to make their own notes.

Notes Pages – prints a slide miniature on each page, together with any notes that you have made to prompt you during your presentation.

Outline View – prints the text of each slide, showing the structure of the presentation.

4 Specify any other options required.

5 Preview your presentation to check how it will look, returning to the **Print** dialog box to adjust if necessary.

6 Click **OK** in the **Print** dialog box to start the printing.

Summary

In this chapter you found out how to create a presentation using PowerPoint. We have discussed:

- The content of a presentation file – slides, handouts, notes, outline
- Adding slides to the presentation
- Slide layout
- Design Templates
- The structure of bullet points
- Charts
- Organization charts
- Tables
- Hide slide, rehearse timings, summary slide, notes, transition effects and slide animation
- Giving a presentation
- Printing the presentation file.

08

information and communication

In this chapter you will learn

- about Internet Explorer
- some ways to use the Internet
- how to keep safe online
- how to browse and to search for information
- how to copy text and pictures from the Web
- how to use Outlook efficiently
- how to organize messages

8.1 Jargon busting

Transferring information via the Internet has become an integral part of our lives, and as this comes with a considerable amount of jargon, we will start off by giving a brief definition of some of the terms you are bound to encounter sooner or later.

The **Internet** is a global network that links millions of computers together. It enables any computer, anywhere in the world, to communicate with any other – as long as they are both connected. It provides the infrastructure that many of us use (and rely on) for global communications.

The **World Wide Web** (WWW or Web) is one way of distributing information over the Internet. It displays the information on web pages, in websites (a group of web pages from the same company or individual).

You can also distribute information over the Internet using email, user groups, instant messaging and file transfer.

When people think or talk about the Internet, they are usually referring to the Web and visiting websites or surfing (browsing around the Web looking for information), but it is important to realize that the Internet and the Web are not the same thing.

Internet Service Provider (ISP): A company that provides you with access to the Internet, e.g. British Telecom, Virgin, Orange.

Web browser: Software used to locate and view web pages, e.g. Internet Explorer, Netscape Navigator, Safari, Firefox.

Web server: A computer on the Internet that stores web pages or provides other services to the Web.

Protocol: A set of rules defining how to do something. Different sets of rules are used for different types of information, e.g.

> **http** (Hyper Text Transfer Protocol) is used for transferring web pages on the Web.

> **ftp** (File Transfer Protocol) is used to transfer files from one computer to another across the Internet.

> **smtp** (Simple Mail Transfer Protocol) is used for transferring emails between servers.

Domain name: The name which identifies the computer on which web pages are stored.

Uniform Resource Locator (URL): The address of a file on the Internet, e.g.

http://www.hodder.co.uk/Category/8725/Computing.htm

http: this identifies the protocol.

// the slashes are separators – double ones after the protocol, and single ones between folders

www.hodder.co.uk/ the domain name

Category/ a folder within the domain

8725/ a folder within the Category folder

Computing.htm a document name (an individual web page)

Domain suffix: Helps you to identify the country and the type of organization that owns a domain. You may notice these:

edu	US educational institution
gov	government agencies
org	non-profit-making organizations
com	US or international commercial organization
co	other commercial organization
net	network organizations
ac	academic institution

Other than for the USA, most URLs will have country codes that identify the organization's base, e.g.

uk (United Kingdom)	fr (France);	de (Germany)
cz (Czech Republic)	dk (Denmark)	es (Spain)
ch (Switzerland)	ca (Canada)	au (Australia).

If there is no country code, it usually indicates that the domain is international or US-based.

Try to work out the type of organization and the location of the following websites, then check them out to see if you were right:

http://www.eastlothian.gov.uk/

http://www.virginmedia.com/

http://www.edinburghrocks.co.uk/

http://www.edinburgh.ac.uk/

http://www.washington.edu/

http://www.nswrno.net.au/

Search engine: A website that allows you to retrieve information from a system using keywords. When using the Internet a search engine will help you locate web pages that contain the keywords that you are looking for.

Cookie: A small text file that is sent from a website to your computer, and stored there. When you revisit the website, your browser will send the text file to it. The main purpose of a cookie is to allow the website to identify the user visiting the site, and perhaps customize the web page content to suit the user's interests and preferences.

Cache: A storage area in your computer's memory used for temporary storage of web pages that you visit in an Internet session. Should you revisit a web page in the same session, you may find that the page loads a lot quicker than it did the first time, as it is being loaded from cache, rather than from the Internet.

Web page: A web page usually contains text, graphics and hyperlinks – and often sounds and perhaps video/movie files.

Hyperlink: A 'hotspot' which could be text or pictures. Hyperlink text is normally (but not always) blue with an underline. With picture hyperlinks, the pointer changes to a hand with a pointing finger on it when you move it over the picture. When you click on a hyperlink you could be taken to another area within the page, or to another web page or a different site.

Website: A number of related web pages, owned and managed by one person or organization.

Really Simple Syndication (RSS): A web feed format used to publish frequently updated content, e.g. blog (web log) entries, news headlines or podcasts. RSS documents, called 'feed', 'web feed' or 'channel', contain either a summary of content from an associated website or the full text. RSS allows people to keep up to date with what is happening on their favourite websites without checking them manually.

Podcast: A digital media file (or a related collection of such files) which is distributed over the Internet to portable media players and PCs using syndication feeds. The word podcast is a fusion of iPod and broadcast as the Apple iPod was the first device that used this technology. You can subscribe to podcasts, which results in you receiving new content from them automatically when it is published. Podcasts are often distributed through RSS.

8.2 Security considerations

As our use of the Internet increases, our exposure to cyber criminals also increases. It can be hard to appreciate just how vulnerable you really are to Internet crime when sitting in the comfort of your home or office, but beware – it is all around you. And there is probably a lot more cyber crime than we ever hear about, as companies prefer not to go public on it in case it affects their business, and individuals might not always report it as they think that they have been a bit naive and it is perhaps their own fault.

If you use social networking sites, e.g. Facebook or Bebo, be very careful about the information you give out and the friends you allow into your space. Think twice before giving out personal information either as part of a business transaction, or on a networking site. If the wrong people get your email address or access to your Facebook area, you may become the victim of online bullying and harassment. We all hear stories in the news about people becoming victims of this – so be very selective when choosing new online 'friends'. And don't give strangers details of your home address, or arrange to meet them because they seem really friendly – anyone can claim to be anybody that they want to be when online. You have no way of checking who they really are. It just isn't worth the risk!

This section will help you become more aware of potential security threats, and give you some guidelines on what you can do to minimize your exposure to those risks when using the Internet.

Downloading files

You will find many sites that allow you to download files from them – text, image, sound and/or video. Downloading simply means you transfer the file from the website that you find it on to your local computer. Downloading files is relatively easy.

Once you have found the file that you want to download, you click on its name or click on a button that says Download or Download Now. You will be asked if you want to Save the file to your local computer, or to Open it from its current location. If you opt to save the file to your local computer, you should check it for viruses before you open it.

Download danger!

Be careful when downloading files – they are often a source of computer viruses – so make sure that the site you are downloading from is one that you believe to be safe.

As well as the virus threat you may be breaking the law yourself when downloading music or videos – so beware!

Virus

A virus is a computer program that gets loaded onto your computer without you realizing it. Once on your computer, it can spread throughout your disks, memory and files and cause all sorts of damage – and many viruses can spread across computer networks and bypass security systems.

Viruses are often spread in email attachments, files that are downloaded from the Internet, and pirate copies of software.

To help protect your system from viruses you should install anti-virus software, e.g. Norton or McAfee. Once installed you must ensure that you keep it up to date (most anti-virus suppliers download updates to your system as they come available) and run it regularly to make sure that your system is clean. You can usually set your virus checker to run automatically at a specific time of day.

Some terms you may encounter when reading about viruses:

Worm: A program which actively transmits itself over a network to infect other computers.

Trojan horse: A piece of software which appears to perform a certain action, but in fact, performs another.

Malware (malicious software): Software designed to infiltrate or damage a computer system without the owner's knowingly consenting to it.

Firewall: Hardware or software device designed to prevent unauthorized access to your computer by other Internet users. The firewall will check all messages entering and leaving your system, and if they don't meet security criteria they will be blocked. Every computer with access to the Internet should have one!

Digital certificate: Identification which can be attached to an email to allow the recipient to verify that the message is really from who it claims to be from. It can also be attached to a website so that the identity of the remote computer can be checked before you conduct a transaction with it (see 'Credit card fraud on the Internet' below).

Encryption: Used to code messages that are sent electronically. The recipient must have the key to the code so that they can decode the message that they receive and read it. If you don't have the key – you can't read the message. Encryption is used when sending sensitive information e.g. credit card details and other private information, and is routinely used by banks and companies that sell goods over the Internet.

Credit card fraud on the Internet

Credit card fraud on the Internet is on the increase. More and more people are buying things online – holidays, wine, tickets for everything from air travel to pop concerts, the weekly shop and car insurance. Most of these transactions cannot take place unless you pay for the service or goods there and then – using your credit card. So it is vitally important that you are as sure as you can be that your details are going to the company you think that you are dealing with, and that no one else can read your details during the transaction.

You should only give private information over the Internet if you are sure that you are connected to a secure site. A secure site is one that takes all reasonable precautions to ensure that the connection or communication between you and them cannot be intercepted by anyone else.

There are several things to indicate that you are on a secure site:

the **Security Report** button to the right of the Address bar. When you click the padlock a dialog box should open giving details of who the security certificate has been issued to, by whom and what its validity period is.

◆ The web address in the address bar should start **https://** to indicate that you are on a secure site.

Computer networks should be secured with user names and passwords. Your IT people will take care of this at work, but you should make sure that you lock your home Internet connection and network down too. If you don't, you are leaving it wide open to abuse – at best you may find neighbours or the students in your stair piggy-backing on your connection (which could slow it down a bit) – or you may find hackers spying on you and collecting your details for their own purposes.

Parental control options

Parents are very aware of the benefits of Internet access for their children. It is a huge information resource for homework and projects, and is great for researching for holidays, and keeping in touch with the grandparents. But it can be a dangerous place. How can parents protect them when they are online? The main options are:

- Supervision – be around when the children are online so that you can see what they are up to (easier with younger ones).

- Web browsing restrictions – you can restrict the websites that children can visit and thereby ensure that they visit only websites that are appropriate for their age.

- Computer games restrictions – you can control access to games, choose an age rating level, etc.

- Computer usage time limits – you can specify when children can log on, and the total hours per day/week.

These options are in the **Tools > Internet Options > Contents** tab.

8.3 First steps...

To open your browser:

1 Open the **Start** menu.

2 Click **Internet Explorer** at the top of the Start menu.

Or

- Click **Launch Internet Explorer Browser** in the Quick Launch area of the Task bar.

If you have a broadband Internet connection you should have immediate access to the Internet when you launch your browser.

If you have a dial-up connection you'll be asked for your user name and password – complete the dialog box when prompted.

The page that appears on your screen when you open your browser application is your home page.

You can visit any page on the Web by entering the URL in the Address bar.

Tabs

If you want to open more than one web page at a time, you can use the tabs that appear along the top of the browser window.

The Internet Explorer screen

The tabs enable you to have several web pages open simultaneously in one browser window – which means that you have only one button on the Task bar for Internet Explorer.

To open a web page on a new tab:

1 Click **New Tab** to the right of the open tabs or press **[Ctrl]-[T]**.

2 Type the URL of the page to go to in the Address bar.

To move from one tab to another:

◆ Just click on the tab you want to view.

To close a tab:

1 Click on the tab you want to close – to bring it to the top.

2 Click the **Close** button on the tab itself.

You must keep at least one tab open.

You could also open a new window so that you can visit another web page without leaving the one that you are viewing.

To open a new window:

- Click the **Page** command button and choose **New Window** from the options (or press **[Ctrl]-[N]**).

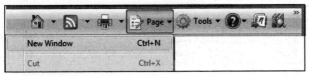

To stop a page from downloading

Some pages can take a while to download. If they have lots of graphics on them, or if your Internet connection is slow for some reason, you may find yourself – waiting – patiently – waiting – patiently... until you don't really want to wait any longer!!

When this happens, you can stop the page, and then move on to some other website.

To stop a page downloading:

- Click ▨ **Stop** to the right of the Address bar.

There may be times when a page downloads, but it doesn't display correctly for some reason. Bits might be missing, or you might know that something has changed but it isn't reflected on screen. When this happens, you should refresh the page.

To refresh a web page:

- Click ↻ **Refresh** to the right of the Address bar or press **[F5]**.

Display/hide images

Most web pages have pictures on them. Some pages are slow to download because of the pictures – the files are so big it takes time to transfer them to your PC. To help speed up the display of your web pages, you can turn the graphics off.

To switch off graphics:

1 Click the **Tools** command and choose **Internet Options**.

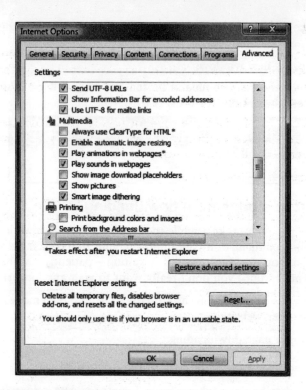

2 Select the **Advanced** tab.

3 In the **Multimedia** area, deselect the **Show pictures** option (and/or **Play animations in web pages**, or **Play sounds in web pages** as required).

♦ You can still display an individual picture or animation on a web page even if you have deselected **Show pictures**. Right-click on its icon and select **Show Picture**.

4 If the pictures on the current page are still visible after you clear the **Show pictures** checkbox, click **Refresh**.

♦ If you wish to set up your system to display pictures again, repeat steps 1–3, selecting the checkboxes required.

To close the web browser:

♦ Click the **Close** button at the right of the title bar.

8.4 Home page

The home page is the one that is displayed when you open your browser or when you click the Home page button on the Toolbar. You could have one page as your home page, or, if you prefer, you can have a set of pages.

You can specify the home page (or pages). You could use your favourite search engine, your own web page, your company website – or all of them – whatever you prefer.

To change the home page:

1 Display the page you want to use for your home page (if you want more than one, open each page on a separate tab).

2 Click the arrow beside the **Home page** button .

3 Select **Add or Change Home Page...**

4 Choose the option required from the dialog box.

> **Add or Change Home Page** ___ X
>
> **Would you like to use the following as your home page?**
> http://news.bbc.co.uk/
>
> ⦿ Use this webpage as your only home page
> ⦿ Add this webpage to your home page tabs
> ⦿ Use the current tab set as your home page
>
> [Yes] [No]

- **Use this webpage as your only home page** – select this option to specify the current web page as your home page.

- **Add this webpage to your home page tabs** – if you already have a home page (or pages) use this option to add another page to them.

- **Use the current tab set as your home page** – if you have several tabs open with different web pages displayed on them, use this option to select them all as your home page setting.

5 Click **OK**.

8.5 Viewing web pages offline

If you find a web page that you want to be able to view or print later, when you are not connected to the Internet, you should save it.

To save a web page:

1 Click the drop-down arrow beside the **Page...** tool.

2 Choose **Save As...**

3 Specify the drive/folder that you want the page on.

4 Accept or edit the filename.

5 Specify the **Save as type** option – the default is *Web Archive, single file MHT*.

6 Click **Save**.

New Window	Ctrl+N
Cut	Ctrl+X
Copy	Ctrl+C
Paste	Ctrl+V
Save As...	
Send Page by E-mail...	
Send Link by E-mail...	
Edit	
Zoom	▶
Text Size	▶
Encoding	▶
View Source	
Security Report	
Web Page Privacy Policy...	

When you are offline, you can still view and/or print the page that you saved.

To view/print the page when offline:

1 Open the file – browse through your folders for it and double-click on it.

2 View/print as required.

8.6 Help

To open Internet Explorer Help:

♦ Click [icon] on the command bar or press **[F1]**.

The Windows Help and Support window will open, at Internet Explorer at a Glance.

♦ You could browse through the Help pages from here.

Or

- Enter details of something you want to search for in the Search field, e.g. 'set home page'.

Or

- Click the **Browse Help** tool and look through the contents to see what might be useful – see *Internet*, *Going online* and *Using the web*.

See section 2.7 for more information on using Windows Help and Support.

8.7 Browser settings

There are a number of different settings that you can change within your browser window.

Toolbars

There are several bars that you can switch on or off, e.g. Links, Status bar and a Menu bar within the browser window.

To switch a bar on or off:

1 Right-click on a blank area in the Command bar at the top of the web page.

2 Click on the bar that you want to show or hide in the shortcut menu.

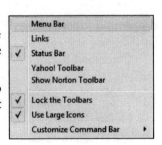

Lock the toolbars

If the toolbars are not locked in position, you will see a line of dots at the left edge of each. You can adjust the amount of space allocated to the toolbar by dragging this line – the mouse pointer changes to a double-headed arrow when it is over it.

- To toggle the locked status, click the **Lock the Toolbars** option in the shortcut menu.

Customize Command bar

You can customize the Command bar.

To control how the icons are displayed:

1 Right-click on the Command bar to display the shortcut menu.

2 Click **Customize Command Bar.**

3 Select a display option – **Show All Text Labels, Show Selective Text** or **Show Only Icons.**

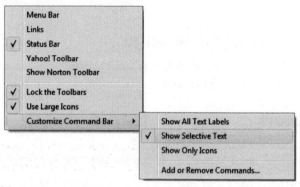

To add or remove commands:

1 Right-click on the Command bar and select **Customize Command Bar.**

2 Click **Add or Remove Commands...**

3 Select the commands that you wish to add (in **Available toolbar buttons**) or remove (in **Current toolbar buttons**).

4 Click **Add** or **Remove** as necessary.

5 Close the dialog box.

8.8 Web navigation

If you know the URL of the web page or site that you require you can easily go to it.

1 Enter its URL in the **Address** field.

2 Press [Enter].

Hyperlinks

Many of the pages that you visit will have hyperlinks to other pages or sites that you may be interested in. As you jump from one location to another, following the hyperlinks, you are surfing the Net.

♦ Click a hyperlink to jump to the location that it points to.

If you want to revisit pages:

♦ Click **Back** and **Forward** to move between the pages you've already visited.

Or

♦ Click the **Recent Pages** arrow and select the URL of the page to return to.

Or

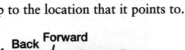

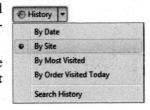

♦ Click the drop-down arrow to the right of the Address bar and select the URL you want to revisit.

As you browse the Web, your browser will store details of where you have been in its History. Your computer will also store Temporary Internet Files so that the web pages can be displayed again quickly if you go back to them.

To display a history of where you have been:

1 Click the **Recent Pages** button and select **History** (or press [Ctrl]-[Shift]-[H]).

2 Click the drop-down arrow to the right of the **History** button to select the order to display the pages in.

3 Click on the page that you wish to revisit.

To clear the history list:

1 Click **Tools** on the Command bar.

2 Select **Delete Browsing History...**

3 Click **Delete history...** and then click **Yes** at the prompt.

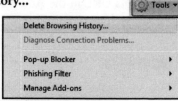

Temporary Internet Files (copies of web pages stored locally for faster viewing) can also be deleted from this dialog box.

Popups and cookies

Popups are a form of online advertising intended to increase web traffic or capture email addresses. If you find them annoying you can block them.

To turn on the Popup Blocker:

1 Click **Tools** and choose **Internet Options**.

2 Display the **Privacy** tab.

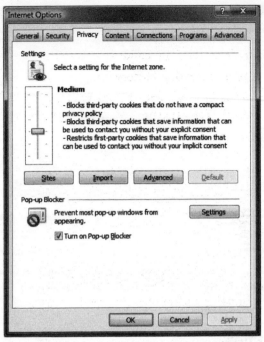

3 Select **Turn on Pop-up Blocker** in the **Pop-up Blocker** area.

4 Click **OK**.

Cookies are small text files that some sites put on your computer to identify you when you revisit their site. You can specify whether or not you wish to accept cookies from a website in the Settings area on the Privacy tab.

8.9 Web searching

If you don't know the URL of a page you will need to search for it. If you are looking for information on a topic you would search for it. The result of a search is a list of several (sometimes thousands) of pages or sites that you may be interested in.

To search for something:

1 Enter a keyword or keywords into the **Instant Search** field on the right of the Address bar.

orkney short break	🔎 ▾

2 Press [**Enter**].

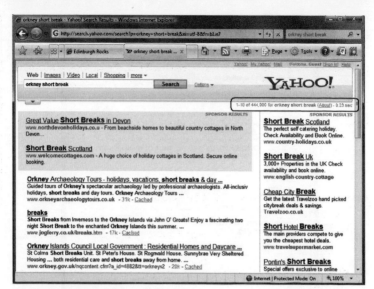

Your search results will be displayed (this search has found 444,000 results!).

Search tips

You can specify which keywords you wish to include or omit from your search by using some basic operators.

For example, if you are looking for restaurants in Edinburgh, but not Chinese ones, you could enter into the search field:

+Edinburgh +Restaurant -Chinese

+ means that the page must contain that word

- means that the page must not.

Search engines

Try some of the many search engines. Start with these:

Google (www.google.co.uk)

AltaVista (www.altavista.com)

Yahoo! (www.yahoo.com)

AskJeeves (www.ask.co.uk)

Excite (www.excite.com).

Most search engines have a directory to allow you to locate the information you require by working through the various topics. However, if you know what you're looking for it's usually quicker to search. You can specify the keywords and phrases that you are looking for in the Search: field (or Search the web: or something similar).

In this example the search is for short breaks in Speyside. Sites that have details of camping are not required, but I want to find sites that mention skiing.

You will notice that:

- Phrases are enclosed within double quotes, e.g. "short breaks".

- Words that should be included are preceded by a plus, e.g. +Speyside.

- Words that should be excluded are preceded by a minus, e.g. -camping.

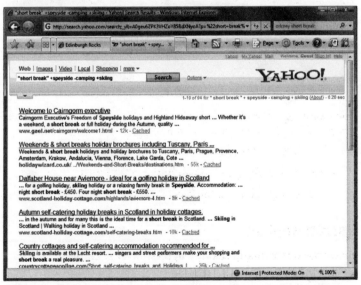

Look through the list of sites found – you may find you have millions of them (if this is the case you need to be much more precise in stating your search requirements).

Web-based encyclopaedias and dictionaries

You may have noticed that there is quite a lot of jargon and terminology associated with computer and Internet use. As the area is developing at an ever-increasing rate, new terms are always appearing. When you come across a term you don't understand you may find an explanation in an online encyclopaedia or dictionary. There are several, the best known being Wikipedia at http://www.wikipedia.org. Wikipedia is available in several languages, and contains definitions of just about anything you can think of – not just on computers or the Internet.

To use Wikipedia:

1 Go to http://www.wikipedia.org.

2 Click **English** to access the English version.

3 Type the word you are looking for into the Search field.

4 Click **Go**.

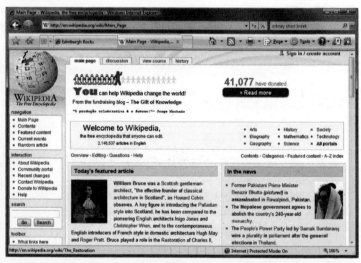

Beware! Wikipedia gives very accessible explanations of a huge range of words and concepts, but don't rely on it alone for information for your school or college research paper. Check out other resources to verify the information that you find before you quote it as gospel in your submissions!

- You will also find a selection of online dictionaries that you can use – do a search for them!

8.10 Favorites

The Favorites Center, on the Explorer bar, contains three different areas – Favorites, Feeds or History.

To display the Favorites:

1 Click [★] **Favorites** at the left of the bar.

2 Select **Favorites**.

To pin the Center open:

Click [◄]

To close the Center:

Click [✕].

If you find a site that you know you will want to revisit, you should add it to your list of Favorites. You can then access the site easily without having to enter the URL or search for it.

To add a page to Favorites:

1 Display the page that you want to add to your Favorites list.

2 Click [★] at the left of the bar then **Add to Favorites** from the list of options.

3 Edit the page name in the **Name** field if you wish.

4 Select the folder that you want to add your page to – leave it at *Favorites*, or click the drop-down arrow and choose a folder from the list.

5 Click **Add**.

To go to a page in your Favorites list:

1 Display the Favorites Center.

2 Open the folder that contains your favorite.

3 Click on the page required.

As you use the Internet your Favorites list will probably get larger. If necessary you can set up folders to help you organize your favorites, and move or delete them to tidy up the list. You can perform these tasks in the Organize Favorites area.

To open the Organize Favorites area:

1 Click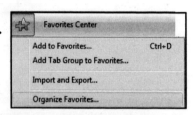

2 Click **Organize Favorites...**

To create a new folder:

1 Click **New Folder**.

2 Give your folder a name.

3 Press [Enter].

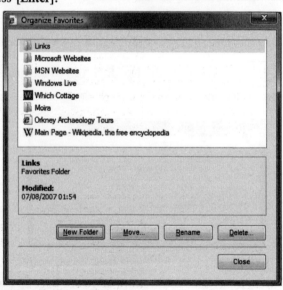

To rename a folder or favorite:

1 Select it.

2 Click **Rename**.

3 Type in a new name and press [**Enter**].

Move a folder or favorite:

1 Select it.

2 Click **Move...**

3 Select the folder you wish to move it to.

4 Click **OK**.

To delete a folder or favorite:

1 Select it.

2 Click **Delete**.

3 Click **Yes** to confirm the deletion.

To view the properties of a favorite:

1 Select the favorite.

2 Read the properties in the lower part of the dialog box.

♦ Close the **Organize Favorites** dialog box when you've finished.

8.11 Copying text and pictures

If you find a web page that contains information that would be useful for a report, paper or essay that you are working on you can easily collect the information into a Word document. As you work you may collect information from many different sources and add them to your document.

To copy text:

1 Select the text that you require from a web page.

2 Right-click within the selected area and then click on **Copy**.

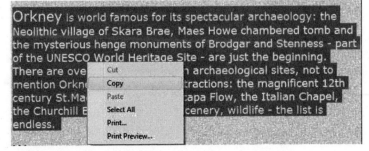

3 Go to or open Word.

4 Open or create a document to paste your text into.

5 Position the insertion point where you want the text to appear.

6 Click the **Paste** tool.

You can add more information to your document as you find it, edit the text, save the document and print it as required.

To copy a picture:

1 Right-click on the picture.

2 Click on **Copy**.

3 Go to the file that you want the copy to appear in.

4 Paste the picture.

Plagiarism

Be aware of plagiarism when using information from the Web (using other people's work and passing it off as your own). Other people's work can be a useful resource, but you should acknowledge your sources. Do a search on plagiarism to find out more. And remember, your teachers and lecturers are probably using plagerism-detection software to check any papers submitted electronically.

8.12 Printing

You may find a web page that you want to print, e.g. one giving confirmation of an order you have placed. There may be a Print button on the page itself – if so all you need to do is click it. Alternatively, you could check the Page Setup, preview the page and print in much the same way as in other applications.

Page Setup

To check/change the Page Setup options:

1 Click the down arrow beside the **Print** command button.

2 Choose **Page Setup...**

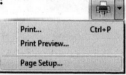

Print...   Ctrl+P
Print Preview...
Page Setup...

3 Edit the fields as required, e.g. change orientation, paper size or margins.

4 Click **OK**.

Print Preview

To preview a page before printing:

1 Click the down arrow beside the **Print** command button.

2 Choose **Print Preview...**

Print

To print a page:

1 Click the **Print** command button to print one copy of the page.

Or

2 Click the down arrow beside the **Print** command button.

3 Choose **Print...** to open the Print dialog box.

4 Set the **Print** options, e.g. **All, Page range, Selection, Frame, Number of copies,** etc.

5 Click **OK**.

8.13   Online forms

If you are booking a holiday, placing an order for goods or signing up for membership of some group using the Web you will be asked to complete an online form.

Completing an online form is usually very straightforward.

It will consist of:

+ Text boxes, so that you can type information in.

+ Drop-down lists, often used so that you can choose from a longish list of options.

+ Radio buttons and checkboxes, to allow you to select from a limited range of options.

Your contact details

Title	Mrs ▼ *
Your first name	Moira *
Your last name	Stephen *
Address	14 Dream Avenue *
Address (continued)	
Town or city	Neverland *
Postcode (ZIP code)	NL15 1PQ *
Your country	United Kingdom ▼ *
Telephone	01234 567 890
Mobile phone	

I am most interested in flights departing from:

☑ Aberdeen	☐ Lanzarote (Arrecife)
☐ Alicante	☐ Lisbon
☐ Almeria	☐ Liverpool
☐ Amsterdam	☐ Ljubljana
☐ Asturias	☑ London Gatwick
☐ Athens	☐ London Luton

Near the end of the form there will be a button that says:

♦ **Send** or **Submit** if the information is being sent over the Internet – click the button when you are finished.

Or

♦ **Print** – if you are meant to print the completed form out and post or fax it.

And usually another which says:

♦ **Reset** – to clear the form.

8.14 Email

How did we live without email? It's one of the quickest, cheapest ways to communicate (once you've got yourself set up with a computer with Internet access).

The convenience and flexibility of email makes it a very attractive communication media. You can send your messages at a time that suits you, and read the messages that you've received. Even if you are in a different time zone from those you communicate with, you don't need to wake anyone up in the middle of the night to talk to them – just send them an email and they'll get it when they next log on.

If you have a web-based email account, you can send and receive your messages from anywhere in the world with Internet access – handy for those who globetrot! It has to be one of the best ways to keep in touch with family, friends and colleagues (next to meeting them for lunch!). There are several web-based email providers to choose from, and some of these offer a free service.

Email fundamentals

Email addresses

These follow the format: user@domain. You will be given an email address from your ISP, company, school, etc. Examples might be john.smith@abc.co.uk or j.f.dupleix@feic.com

Email systems

There are two main types of email system – those that are web-based (and often free), e.g. Yahoo!, Hotmail; and those that you pay for, e.g. Outlook, Virgin, Quistanet.

The main advantages of a web-based service is that it is usually free and can be accessed easily from anywhere in the world with an Internet connection. One of the main disadvantages is often the amount of storage allocation you are given (although you can often get more if you pay for it).

Services that you subscribe to have the obvious disadvantage of cost – but they often give you a greater range of facilities and more storage space.

If you don't already have an email account, and would like to have a free web-based one, it's worth visiting **http://www.free-email-address.com/** to get a comparison of the current offerings.

Network etiquette (netiquette)

In all walks of life, good manners are appreciated, and email is no exception. When sending emails you should ensure that you:

♦ Complete the **Subject** field with a brief accurate description of what the message is about.

♦ Keep the email short and to the point – no one will appreciate you using up their mailbox storage allocation with rambling messages.

♦ Spell-check the document before you send, to help ensure it doesn't contain errors.

♦ Consider formatting your replies so that the recipient can easily tell the difference between the original message and the reply (it might just be a case of indenting one of them).

Digital signature

A digital signature is a type of cryptography used to simulate the security properties of a signature in digital form. Digital signature schemes normally require two keys, the user's private key for signing and a public key for verifying signatures. The output of the signature process is called the digital signature.

Other forms of electronic communication

Short Message Service (SMS)

The Short Message Service (SMS) is a means of sending short messages to and from mobile phones. Most SMS messages are mobile-to-mobile text messages, though the standard supports other types of broadcast messaging as well.

Voice over Internet Protocol (VoIP)

A Voice over Internet Protocol (VoIP) is a protocol optimized for transmission of voice over the Internet. VoIP is also known as IP telephony, Internet telephony, Broadband telephony, Broadband Phone and Voice over Broadband.

A potential benefit is cost savings due to utilizing a single network to carry voice and data, especially where users have existing underutilized network capacity that can carry VoIP at no additional cost.

Instant Messaging (IM)

Instant messaging allows you to communicate with friends and colleagues in real time. When you access an IM system you can tell which of your contacts are online – you have probably heard of some IM systems, e.g. MSN, Yahoo!, Google Talk. They are low cost, and allow you to transfer files as well as messages.

Virtual communities

An online (virtual) community is one that you may join for a variety of reasons, social, study, research, etc. Social networking sites, e.g. Facebook and Bebo, have become very popular with friends and families that are geographically separate but want to keep up to date with each other regularly. Internet forums allow you to discuss topics of interest with colleagues and peers from around the globe. You can drop into chat rooms to catch up on the gossip with friends and play online games with people you may never meet. Sites like Second Life give you the chance to become a member of a virtual community where you have your own fictitious character and role in the community's life.

Think safe!!

Emails are not a secure way of sending messages. They can be easily intercepted by unscrupulous Internet users! So don't send sensitive information via email. Bank account details, pin numbers – in fact any information that you don't want to fall into the wrong hands – should be transmitted in some other way, e.g. a secure link to your bank.

You may receive emails that look as though they have come from your bank or credit card company suggesting that you click here to contact them and confirm your details. Don't! Banks and credit card companies don't use emails to collect or confirm sensitive data! If you receive this type of email you are probably being targeted by a 'phishing' scam where someone is trying to collect your details so that they can use them to their own advantage.

Phishing is an attempt to criminally and fraudulently acquire sensitive information, such as usernames, passwords and credit card details, by masquerading as a trustworthy entity in an electronic communication (eBay, PayPal and online banks are common targets of phishing scams).

You are also bound to receive some unsolicited email – called 'junk mail' or 'spam' – as people do mass mailings to random email addresses to try to engage you in some activity and relieve you of your funds or personal details. If something looks too good to be true – it probably is. So ignore it, or try to contact the organization some other way to check things out. You will often find that a search on the Internet for information on some offer that looks suspicious will confirm that you were right to be cautious!

Email attachments are another possible danger! If you don't recognize the sender of the message, be very wary of opening any attachments the message contains. It is a favourite way of distributing computer viruses. Many virus checking systems will scan incoming emails and block any that are suspect. But be careful!

If you work for a company, you may find there are guidelines and rules that you must follow when using their email system. So make sure that you know what they are – and follow them. They are there for a reason – to try to ensure the safety and security of the company's staff and systems.

Email is no more dangerous than any other activity – just keep your wits about you! You wouldn't write your pin number on a piece of paper, store it beside your bank card – and leave them lying on the table in your bank (would you?) – so don't be careless online either.

Whatever email system you use, set your security settings to their limit and/or ensure you have up-to-date anti-virus software checking your incoming emails.

If you are part of a virtual community, remember to be careful with your real personal details!

8.15 Introducing Outlook Express

The email service discussed here is Microsoft Outlook Express.

To open Outlook Express:

1 Click the **Start** button.

2 Select **Outlook Express** at the top of the Start menu.

The Outlook Express window

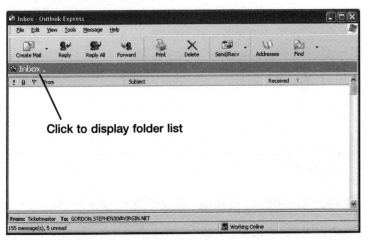

Click to display folder list

8.16 Send email

To send an email:

1 Click **Create New**.

2 Enter the email address of the recipient in the **To:** field.

3 If you wish to send a copy of the message to someone else, enter their address in the **Cc:** field.

4 Type in a **Subject**.

5 Key in your message.

6 Spell-check it – click the **Spelling** tool on the **Message** tab.

• Most messages have normal priority but you can mark a message as High priority (or Low priority) if required – the feature is in the **Options** group on the **Message** tab.

7 Click **Send**.

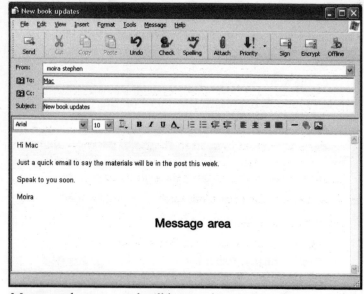

Messages that you send will be saved automatically in your *Sent Items* folder.

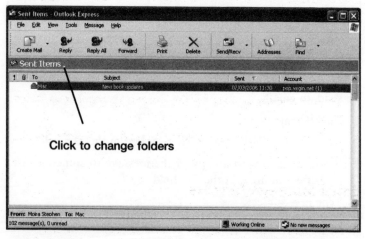

You can save an email message – perhaps because you haven't finished it – and then complete it at a later date. When you save an email, it is put in the *Drafts* folder. To complete the message just open it from the *Drafts* folder, update and send.

To:, Cc: and Bcc:

Type the address of each recipient into the appropriate field (if there is more than one, separate them with a semicolon ;).

- The To: field is for the main recipient(s).

- The Cc: field is for those that you want to send a copy so that they know what's going on.

- The Bcc: field is for sending *blind copies*. Only the message sender and each individual in the Bcc field know that they have been sent a message. Those who have been sent a Bcc will not know who else has been sent a copy.

To show the Bcc field for a message:

1 Create a new message.

2 Choose **All Headers** from the **View** menu.

Subject field

Type the message title in the Subject field – this will be displayed in the Inbox of the recipient, so they have an idea what the message is about.

Message area

Type your message in here.

- You can use the buttons on the formatting toolbar to format your text.

- Spell-check your message before you send it – click the Spelling button on the main toolbar.

Email message formats

Outlook allows you to format your email messages as HTML, RTF or Plain Text. The default format is HTML. Both HTML and RTF allow you to format your messages using different fonts, colour, bullet points, etc. Plain Text just allows – well – plain unformatted text.

Not all email applications allow their users to view formatted messages. So you should write your messages using a format that your recipient's email system supports. **All** email applications support unformatted text – if in doubt, Plain Text is a safe option. It also keeps the mail message smaller.

If you know your recipient is using Outlook (or an application that supports formatting) then the best option to use is HTML. You can then format the text with the usual formatting options.

The format can be changed if required.

1 Open the **Tools** menu and choose **Options**.
2 Select the **Send** tab.
3 Set the **Mail Sending** format.
4 Click **OK**.

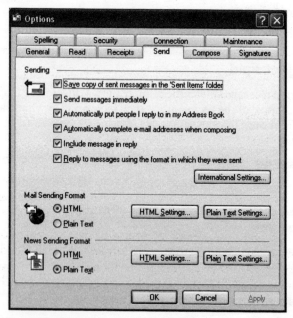

Practise sending messages to some of your friends and family.

Copy and paste

You can copy and paste text from other emails or documents into your email using normal copy and paste routines.

8.17 Attaching a file

You can easily attach files to your email message. You may want to send someone a report or spreadsheet to have a look at, or a picture that you took on holiday. Beware when sending large attachments, e.g. pictures – they can take a while to transmit and fill up your recipient's mailbox!

To attach a file to a message:

1 Enter the address(es) and Subject fields as usual.

2 Click **Attach File** [Attach] on the **Message** tab.

3 Locate the file you wish to attach.

4 Click **Attach**.

5 Repeat 2–4 for each attachment.

◆ Your attachments will be displayed below the Subject field.

6 Enter your message (if you haven't already done so).

7 Spell-check your message.

8 Click **Send**.

Things to remember when sending attachments:

◆ Attachments make your email larger and so it will take longer to send.

◆ If an attachment is too big, the recipient's mailbox may not accept it, or may not have room for it.

◆ The attachment should be of a file type that your recipient can open. There is no point sending them a Word 2007 document if they are using WordPerfect 5.1! You may need to convert the file to a suitable format before you send it (use **File > Save As...** in the application).

◆ Anti-virus software may stop your attachment from reaching the recipient's mailbox – many will not allow an Access database file through.

◆ Network software may also stop your attachment – perhaps because it is too big or of a file type it won't permit.

8.18 Inbox

Messages that you receive will be displayed in your Inbox.

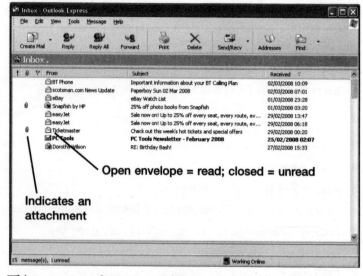

Open envelope = read; closed = unread

Indicates an
attachment

Things to note about your Inbox:

- Unread messages have a closed envelope icon beside them, read messages have an open envelope.

- If you have read a message, then want to mark it as unread again, right-click on it in the Inbox and click **Mark as Unread**. The envelope icon will appear closed again.

- You can sort the messages in your Inbox into ascending or descending order. Click the column heading, **From, Subject, Received** or **Size**, to sort your messages.

- A message with an attachment will have a paperclip icon beside it.

- To open a message to read it – double-click on it.

- You can save the address of the sender from an open message. Right-click on the address and choose **Add to Address Book** from the menu.

| Add to Address Book |
| Find... |
| Block Sender... |
| Copy |
| **Properties** |

- If you get emails from someone that you don't want to receive them from, right-click on the address, then click **Block Sender** The address will be added to the Blocked Senders list.

  You can manage the Blocked Senders list from the Inbox – open the **Tools** menu, choose **Message Rules** and then **Blocked Senders List**.

If the message has an attachment:

- Double-click on the attachment to open it.

Or

To save the attachment:

1 Right-click on it.

2 Click on **Save As...**

3 Specify where you want the file saved and what you want it called.

4 Click **Save**.

Virus danger

Beware of attachments from sources that you do not recognize – they may be carrying viruses. If there is any doubt, don't open it!

8.19 Print a message

You can print a copy of an email if you wish.

1 Open the message.

2 Click **Print Preview** if you wish to preview it.

Or

- Click **Print** to send one copy of the message to the default printer.

If you wish to set any printing options, e.g. number of copies, display the Print dialog box and select the options required.

- To close a message without replying to it, click the **Close** button.

8.20 Reply to/forward a message

You will often want to reply to an email message, or perhaps forward it to someone else.

1 Open the message.

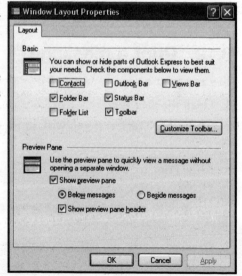

2 Click **Reply** (to reply to the sender only) or **Reply to All** (to send your reply to everyone that the message was sent to).

3 Type in your reply/message and attach any files required.

4 Click **Send**.

To forward a message to someone else:

1 Click **Forward**.

2 Enter the recipient's address details.

3 Carry on from step 3 above.

8.21 Productivity options

Customize window

You can customize the Outlook Express window to suit the way you prefer to work.

1 Open the View menu.

2 Choose **Layout**.

3 Select/deselect the Layout objects as required.

4 Click **OK**.

Customize field display

To customize the list of fields in the folders:

1 Right-click on the column headings.

2 Choose **Columns...**

3 Select, deselect or re-order the fields.

4 Click **OK**.

Send options

At the Inbox window:

1 Open the **Tools** menu and choose **Options**.

2 Select the **Send** tab.

3 Set your Sending options.

4 Click **OK**.

Do you want to include the original message when you send a reply? It's normal to include it in business emails, but not in private ones.

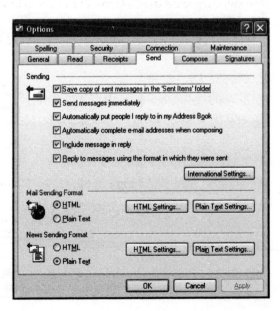

Flag a message

There may be times that you receive or send a message and you know that you want to return to it, perhaps to follow it up or do something else that needs to be done.

To stop you losing track of the message, you can flag it so that your attention is drawn back to it.

To flag a message:

• Click in the flag column for the message, in the Inbox or Sent Items – the message will be red flagged.

To remove the flag from a message:

• Click on the flag in the flag column.

8.22 The Address Book

It is a good idea to put addresses that you will use again into your Address Book. Then you can use them without having to re-key them. You can add addresses when you send or receive a message, or you can enter them manually.

To add an address manually:

1 Open the Address Book – click on **Addresses** on the toolbar in the Inbox.

2 Click **New**.

3 Select **New Contact**.

4 Complete the contact details and click **OK**.

To add an address from incoming mail:

1 Open the mail message – double-click on it.

2 Right-click on the sender's email.

3 Click on **Add to Address Book**.

4 Complete the details as necessary and click **OK**.

Distribution lists

You can set up distribution lists or groups, so that you can quickly add a number of recipients to your emails. This option is useful if you will be sending emails to the same group of people regularly, e.g. your friends, social club or team at work.

1 Open the Address Book.

2 Click **New**.

3 Choose **New Group**.

4 Enter a name for your group.

To select a member from your Address Book:

5 Click **Select Members**.

6 Double-click on each name in the list to add them to the Members field.

7 Click **OK** to close the address list.

8 Click **OK** to save the group.

To send an email to the group:

1 Select the group name from the Address Book. This opens the New Message window, with the group in the To: field.

Or

2 Create a new message.

3 Type the group name into the To: field in your message.

Or

♦ Click [To:] then in the **Select Names** dialog box, double-click on the group name to select it and click **OK**.

4 Complete and send the message in the normal way.

8.23 Signature

An signature allows you to append your standard closure to an email automatically.

You might like to finish your emails with something like:

> With best wishes
>
> Moira

Rather than type this into every message, you can store the text in a signature and get Outlook Express to add this to every email.

To create a signature:

1 Open the **Tools** menu and choose **Options**.

2 Select the **Signatures** tab.

3 Click **New**.

4 Give your signature a name.

5 Enter your signature text in the **Edit Signature** area.

6 Set the options, e.g. *Add signatures to all outgoing messages*.

7 Click **OK**.

To edit an existing signature:

1 Open the **Tools** menu and choose **Options**.

2 Select the **Signatures** tab.

3 Select the signature you want to edit.

4 Update the text in the **Edit Signature** area.

To delete a signature:

1 Select the signature.

2 Click **Remove**.

To rename a signature:

1 Select the signature.

2 Click **Rename**.

3 Enter a new name at the dialog box.

4 Click **OK**.

◆ Next time you compose an email, your signature will be in place already when you start.

8.24 Message management

Once you've started using email, you will probably find that it becomes one of your main ways of communicating with family, friends and colleagues. The number of emails that you send and receive will increase substantially. Eventually, you will get to the stage where you need to sort your emails out – perhaps get rid of some, and put others into folders. You need to get organized!

Searching for mail

You might need to search through your emails to find the one that you are looking for, or if you receive a lot of emails from the same source, or about the same topic, you might want to organize the messages into folders so that you can find them easily.

To search for a message by sender, subject or email content:

1 Click **Find**.

2 Complete the dialog box as required.

3 Click **Find Now**.

To sort your emails:

◆ Click the column heading that you wish to sort on.

The first time you click on the heading, the list will sort in ascending order on that column. Click again and it will sort in descending order.

The Find Message dialog box

Using folders

To create a new folder:

1 Right-click on the folder that will be the parent of the one you are about to create, e.g. *Personal Folders*.

2 Click **New Folder...** to open the **Create New Folder** dialog box.

3 Give your folder a name e.g. *Cabinet*.

4 Click **OK**.

You can create additional folders within this, if you wish to store the messages you send and receive from different individuals or on different topics. Just remember to right-click on the folder that will be the parent of the new folder you are creating.

To move messages to a folder:

1 Right-click on the message – probably one in your *Inbox* or *Sent Items* folder.

2 Click on **Move to Folder...**

3 Select the folder to move the message to.

4 Click **OK**.

**Moving a
message using
the dialog box**

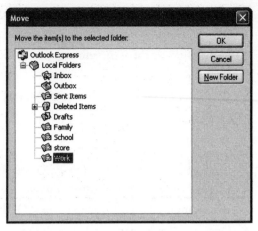

To rename:

1 Right-click on the folder to open the menu.

2 Click on **Rename** *folder name*.

3 Type the new name and press **[Enter]**.

To move a folder:

1 Right-click on the folder and select **Move** *folder name*.

2 Select the folder you want to move it to and click **OK**.

To copy a folder:

1 Right-click on the folder and select **Copy** *folder name*.

2 Select the folder you want to copy it to and click **OK**.

To delete a folder:

1 Right-click on the folder and select **Delete** *folder name*.

Or

♦ Select it and press **[Delete]**.

To delete a message:

♦ Select the message in a folder and press **[Delete]**.

Or

♦ If the message is open, click **Delete** on the toolbar.

The deleted message is put in your *Deleted Items* folder. If you
delete accidentally, you can recover it from here (provided the
folder hasn't been emptied).

To restore a deleted message:

1 Select *Deleted Items* to display its contents.

2 Right-click on the item you want to recover.

3 Click on **Move to Folder...**

4 Select the folder (or create a new one) and click **OK**.

The *Deleted Items* folder should be emptied regularly.

To manually empty it:

1 Right-click on *Deleted Items* in the Navigation pane.

2 Click on **Empty Deleted Items Folder.**

To empty the folder each time you exit Outlook Express:

1 Open the **Tools** menu and choose **Options**.

2 Display the **Maintenance** tab.

3 Select **Empty messages from the 'Deleted Items' folder on exit.**

4 Click **OK**.

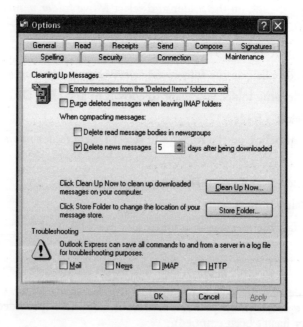

Summary

In this chapter you have learnt how to:

+ Access the Internet
+ Locate a website or page using a URL
+ Specify your home page
+ Use the Help system
+ Save a web page to disk
+ Change your toolbar display
+ Display/hide images on a web page
+ Use hyperlinks to jump from one page to another
+ Search the Web for sites and pages
+ Add a URL to your Favorites folder
+ Copy information from a web page into a file
+ Print a web page
+ Fill in an online form
+ Create, send and read email messages
+ Cut/copy and paste text from one message to another or from a different file into your email message
+ Attach a file to an email message
+ Open or save an attachment
+ Print a message
+ Reply to an email message
+ Add, delete and edit contacts in your Address Book
+ Add a signature to your message
+ Manage your messages.

taking it further

Sound basic PC skills are useful on many different levels – personal, educational and vocational. Now that you have improved your PC skills, why not consider going for certification? The challenge of an exam can be fun, and a recognized certificate may improve your job prospects.

You might want to consider MOS exams (Microsoft Office Specialist) or ECDL (European Computer Driving Licence) or the SQA (Scottish Qualifications Authority) PC Passport, or the new CLAIT exams.

Visit:

- www.microsoft.com/learning for more on MOS
- www.ecdl.com for information on ECDL
- www.sqa.org.uk for SQA certificates
- www.new-clait.co.uk/ for CLAIT.

If you want to extend your knowledge of the software introduced in this book why not try the other Teach Yourself books in the series:

- *Teach Yourself Windows XP*
- *Teach Yourself Word*
- *Teach Yourself Excel*
- *Teach Yourself Access*
- *Teach Yourself PowerPoint*
- *Teach Yourself the Internet*

Wishing your every success with your PC!

teach
yourself

basic computer skills
Windows Vista edition
moira stephen

- Are you new to computers?
- Do you want an accessible, jargon free guide?
- Would you like to master the basic applications?

Basic Computer Skills Windows Vista Edition is perfect for any new computer user who wants to get up and running quickly and simply. With step-by-step instructions and minimal jargon, this book will ensure that you quickly gain a clear understanding of all the key applications on your computer. Covering Windows Vista, Office 2007, Internet Explorer 7 and more, this is the must-have beginner's guide to computing.

Moira Stephen is a former college lecturer and IT consultant, as well as being a prolific author of computing books.

teach yourself

Word 2007
moira stephen

- Are you new to Word?
- Do you want to produce great-looking documents?
- Do you need to brush up your word processing skills?

Word 2007 is a comprehensive guide to this word processing application that is suitable for all beginners. From document creation through to templates and mail merge, it progresses steadily from the basics to more advanced features and includes time-saving shortcuts and practical advice. With its clear approach and numerous illustrations it will prove an invaluable resource to all Word users.

Moira Stephen is a former college lecturer and IT consultant, as well as being a prolific author of computing books.